D0829263

REAL KIDS
REAL ADVENTURES

Ready for more real adventures?
Look for these other exciting volumes in your
favorite bookstore:

Alex Golden

REAL KIDS
REAL ADVENTURES
TRUE STORIES BY DEBORAH MORRIS

NUMBER 5

OVER THE EDGE

KIDNAPPED!

SWEPT UNDERGROUND

BROADMAN
& HOLMAN
PUBLISHERS

Nashville, Tennessee

Published by:
Broadman & Holman Publishers

Design: Steven Boyd

4240-55
0-8054-4055-0

Dewey Decimal Classification: JSC
Subject Heading: Courage \ Faith \ Survival
Librar· of Congress Card Catalog Number: 94-11741

Library of Congress Cataloging-in-Publication Data
Morris, Deborah, 1956–
    Real kids, real adventures.

    1. Christian biography—United States—Juvenile
literature 2. Children—United States—Biography—
Juvenile literature. [1. Survival. 2. Adventure and
adventurers. 3. Christian biography.]
I. Title

BR1714. M67   1995
209'.2'27'3 [B]
ISBN 0-8054-4051-8 (v. 1)   94-11741 CIP

To my lovely and talented mother-in-law,
Anne Morris,
who told me I had to become a writer
or she'd yell at me.

Acknowledgments

Many thanks to Sergeant Tom Armstrong of the El Monte Police Department for his help with fact checking "Kidnapped!"

Also thanks to Detective Rob Sherwood for helping bring Raymond Lauriano back to his family.

David James at home in British Columbia, Canada

Over the Edge

The David James Story

"When am I going to get to see your new gold mine, Oopa?" David James asked his grandfather across the dinner table. "I've really been wanting to go there."

Bud Ryckman, a tall, broad-shouldered man with white hair and brown eyes, smiled. "It's not a gold mine yet, David, just a gold *claim*. That means I've been given the OK to look for gold there. It's in pretty rough country, though. I'm not sure about taking along a young lad like you."

1

David rolled his eyes. "I think I could handle it. I'm not a baby, you know. And you said I might be able to help this time with the line cut." A line cut is where gold prospectors clear away trees and brush around the edges of a mining claim.

"Well," Mr. Ryckman said doubtfully, "I'll think about it. But in the meantime, how about a quick fishing trip this weekend?"

"Sure!" David flashed an impish grin that showed his silver braces. "I'll call Mum and Dad to let them know I won't be home."

David was fifteen but very small for his age. People often thought he was twelve or thirteen. He lived with his grandparents during the week so he could go to school in West Vancouver, but on weekends he usually went home.

His parents, twin brothers, and two little sisters lived about forty-five minutes away in Pitt Meadows. West Vancouver and Pitt Meadows are both towns in British Columbia, Canada.

Now, in June, David was in summer school. He hadn't done very well in French during the school year, mainly because he hated the subject. But in Canada, where both French and English are spoken, students are required to learn it. David had to retake French before he could start eleventh grade in the fall.

At the mention of a fishing trip, Mrs. Ryckman winked at David. "Are you sure you want to go fishing with Oops again? You know what happened last time!"

"Oops" and "Oopa" were both silly names for Mr. Ryckman. When David was just two or three, his grandfather had brought him some tiny *lederhosen* (a type of shorts) from Germany. When he told David that in German, "grandfather" is *Opa*, David had liked the way it sounded. From that day on, he called his grandfather Opa. It gradually turned into Oopa and Oops.

Mr. Ryckman gave his wife a pained look. "You'd better watch it, woman," he threatened, shaking a fork at her. "It wasn't my fault we ran out of gas that time. The chaps at the boat place were supposed to have filled our extra tank."

David shoved his chair away from the table, tilting it backward at an alarming angle. "But *you're* the one who's always lecturing about boating safety and stuff, Oopa," he said sternly. "You know, all that stuff about staying alert and being responsible. Then you go and get us stuck way out in the ocean!"

The incident had happened several months earlier. David and Mr. Ryckman had gone out fishing one morning in a small rented boat. But around noon, when they decided to go back for lunch, they discovered that their extra gas tank was empty. They only made it halfway back to shore before the engine sputtered and died, leaving them drifting along with the ocean current.

They had both yelled and waved frantically until somebody on a huge yacht spotted them and threw them a line. The yacht towed them back to shore, dragging them through the waves like a little toy boat on a string. It had all been really embarrassing.

Mr. Ryckman held up both hands in surrender. "OK, OK. I should've double-checked the extra gas can. But if we're going to talk about being responsible . . . " He gave his grandson a meaningful look. "Seems I could bring up a certain person's French grade."

David let his chair settle back down with a thump. "Uh, no, that's OK, Oopa," he said hastily. "Let's change the subject."

"I thought you might feel that way," Mr. Ryckman said smugly. "Now, if you're done with your dinner, let's go out to the garage and start getting our fishing stuff together."

David and his grandfather had always spent a lot of time together. Mr. Ryckman wasn't like a lot of grandfathers. He might be sixty-three, but he wasn't *old*. He had been a professional football player when he was younger, and he still liked playing rugby. He had been David's rugby coach in eighth grade.

Mr. Ryckman was adventurous too. He came from a whole family of pioneer gold prospectors. He loved tramping through wild, unexplored areas with his rock hammer and gold pan. Over his lifetime he had staked almost fifty mining claims.

"Years ago, during the big California Gold Rush," he liked to tell David, "my great-grandparents left England and came to America with another family to try their luck. My grandmother was just a girl then.

By the time they got to San Francisco, the gold rush was over, but then they heard rumors about a gold strike here in British Columbia. The two families walked all the way from California to Idaho and then came the rest of the way by river. By the time they got to Canada, my grandmother had fallen in love with a boy from the other family. They got married in a town not far from here."

He always had stories like that to tell—sometimes too many. He could lecture for hours about trees, or history, or animals, or any other subject that came up. David sometimes got tired of listening, but it was nice to have a grandfather who was smart. He always knew the answers to almost any question you could ask.

They decided to leave for their fishing trip that Friday as soon as David got out of school. That morning, David had an even harder time than usual paying attention to his French teacher, Monsieur Whoever. There were about three million things he would rather be doing than repeating, *"Je m'appelle David James. Comment allez-vous?"* (My name is David James. How are you?)

But he knew he'd be in serious trouble if he flunked French again. He was already a little worried. He was only allowed one absence the whole summer, and he had stayed home sick once already. If he missed even one more day, he would fail.

When the bell rang at noon, David raced home, happily replacing French thoughts with fish thoughts. "Grandma! Oopa!" he shouted as he dashed into the house. "I'm home!"

"Oopa's out in the garage," Mrs. Ryckman called. David followed her voice into the kitchen and found her standing at the counter. "I'm making some sandwiches and things for you to take along," she said.

David grinned. "Good! And can you put in some of those sausages I like? Oopa can cook them when we get to the motel, since he doesn't like eating out."

"I know. I guess I've spoiled him, eh?" She smiled. "I'll put in some bacon and tomato sandwiches and a few sausages. You'd better catch some fish tomorrow, though, or you'll starve."

"Don't worry, we will."

"Starve, or catch fish?"

"Catch fish," David responded with a grin. "The salmon should be running."

Wandering out to the garage, David found his grandfather bending over his tackle box. "Hi, Oopa," he said. "Ready to go?"

"Almost. So, how'd school go today?"

David made a face. "Just great. French was so much fun I could hardly stand it." At least the last part was true!

Mr. Ryckman laughed. "Well, why don't we start carrying our gear out to the car? I'll grab the cooler from Grandma."

He closed his tackle box and straightened his back. "We need to hit the road. We don't want to miss the two o'clock ferry."

Whales and Fish Tales

The B. C. ferry, the *Spirit of British Columbia*, was just ten minutes away at Horseshoe Bay. It was a huge, white boat with rows and rows of little windows along the sides. When they got to the dock, Mr. Ryckman drove up the ramp onto the ferry. Inside, it looked like a three-story parking garage. They parked and got out.

Some people sat in the small cafeteria the whole time, but David preferred to wander around the deck. Several times he had spotted porpoises or interesting fish in the water.

At two o'clock sharp the ferry whistle blew, signaling that they were about to leave. The trip out to Campbell River, where they would be staying, would take two hours. David leaned on the rail as they slowly pulled away from the dock. Horseshoe Bay looked beautiful from the water. The jagged coast was lined with huge mountains, evergreen forests, and steep rock cliffs. In many places, the ocean ran right up to the bottom of the mountains.

"So," Mr. Ryckman said, leaning his elbows on the rail, "how many salmon do you think you'll catch this time out?"

"Only one," David said seriously, "but it'll weigh fifty pounds and be six feet long. I've decided to leave all the little ones for you this time."

Mr. Ryckman nodded slowly. "Righto. But we're only renting a little twelve-foot boat, eh? A fish that big, it might sink us."

"Then we'll just have to tow it in. Like that yacht towed us when we ran out of gas. Remember?"

The older man winced. "I'd rather not." He glanced out at the water, and then his eyes widened. "Hey, look at that!"

David squinted, wondering if his grandfather was playing a joke. "I don't see anything."

"Look, right there!" He pointed out at the water. "See it?"

This time, David did. About five hundred yards away, a tall black fin was slowly rising from the water. Even at that distance, it looked huge. It glided along for a moment and then disappeared from sight.

"Wow!" David yelled. "What was that?" Several other people crowded around the boat rail, pointing.

"A male killer whale!" Mr. Ryckman said excitedly. "See how the water is disturbed in a big area out there? I'll bet there's a whole pod!" Pods are groups of killer whales. "A male usually has a bunch of females and young whales following along. The females' dorsal fins are a lot smaller, but if you keep watching you might see them too." He pointed. "Look! It's surfacing again!"

The black dorsal fin rose again until it was standing more than five feet out of the water. As it glided across the waves like a distant sailboat mast, a faint mist suddenly rose above the water. It sank out of sight again.

"Did you see the spout?" Mr. Ryckman asked. "That came from his blowhole. Killer whales breathe air, just like we do. They have to come up every few minutes to blow out and get a new breath."

"Yeah, I know, Oopa," David said quickly. With his grandfather, the simplest subjects could turn into long lectures. "We learned all about killer whales in school, and—"

But Mr. Ryckman wasn't even listening. "Fifteen or twenty Orca can travel in a pod, and some of them can be twenty or thirty feet [6 or 9 meters] long!"

David sighed. Once his grandfather got started on a subject, it was no use trying to stop him. "Pretty big," he murmured, keeping his eyes glued to the water. He only half listened as his grandfather went on and on. He wished the pod would swim closer. He'd never seen a killer whale up close.

"Did you know that killer whales are members of the dolphin family?" Mr. Ryckman continued. "They feed on seals and fish and even other whales. They can kill almost anything, even a Great White shark. Once, I watched a pod pick off a whole seal colony. Those huge whales came roaring right out of the water onto the rocks and grabbed the seals one by one. I'd never seen anything like it."

"Uh-huh." David was disappointed that the male hadn't come up again. Had he headed back out to sea?

Just as he thought he must have disappeared for good, the tall black fin appeared again, now only four hundred yards away. He *was* getting closer!

"Killer whales are smart too," his grandfather was saying. "They're not afraid of anything. Did I ever tell you the story about the time one came right up to our boat when Grandma and I were out fishing?"

That finally got David's attention. "What? A whale came up to your boat? What happened?"

Mr. Ryckman looked pleased. He always liked it when somebody *asked* for a story. It didn't happen very often.

"Well," he said, warming up, "we were out in a little twelve-foot aluminum boat one day, just fishing and enjoying the sunshine. All of a sudden, there was this sound like a gunshot right next to us. *Pow!* Just like that, out of nowhere." He shook his head, remembering. "Your grandma screamed. We both whirled around and saw this male killer whale maybe six feet away from our boat. The sound was him blowing out his spout."

David's eyes were wide. "What did you do?"

"Well, we just sat there, afraid to move. I was thinking how easy it would be for him to knock our boat over just by bumping it. He was a good thirty feet long! And even though killer whales are usually friendly to people, I was afraid if we fell in the water he might mistake us for seals or something. And I'd already seen what they can do to seals."

"So what happened?" David asked. He glanced out at the water again, this time a little more wary.

"Well, after a second he kind of rolled sideways in the water and brought one eye up to take a look at us. Like I said, killer whales are very smart. He must have been curious about us. Anyway, he just stared at us for a second with that big eye, and then he was gone, just like that." He snapped his fingers for emphasis.

"Did he ever come back?"

"No. I guess he'd seen enough to tell that we didn't look like food. Once he decided to leave, he didn't waste any time. They're fast, you know."

"How fast?"

"Oh, I'd say they can swim about twenty or twenty-five miles [32 to 40 kilometers] per hour," Mr. Ryckman said. He looked down at the water rushing along the sides of the boat. "About the same speed we're moving right now, or maybe a little faster."

David drummed his fingers on the rail. Suddenly it didn't seem like such a good idea after all for the whales to swim up to the ferry. "Do killer whales ever attack boats?"

"No, no. They're like really big dolphins. They're playful. I've seen them jump way up out of the water and spin around just for fun or do a series of fast body rolls. In fact, a lot of the killer whales Sea World trains for their shows come from this area."

"Really? I bet they're hard to catch!"

Mr. Ryckman chuckled. "Not really. Years ago, a chap I knew caught one. He had a permit to kill one to study, but he accidentally harpooned it through the blubber on its back instead of through its body. When he tugged on the harpoon rope, the whale just turned around and started following him! He ended up leading it back over twenty miles, right into a pen. He named it Hound Dog because it followed him home like a dog on a leash."

"What did he do with it?" David asked.

"Well, as soon as he got Hound Dog into the pen, the other whales in the pod started swimming back and forth out in the ocean, yapping and calling to him. Killer whales can chatter really loud, like dolphins. Turned out Hound Dog's pod had followed him the whole way."

"So did he let Hound Dog go?"

"No, I think Hound Dog went to live in a big aquarium here in Canada. I heard he ended up dying from an infection."

"How long do killer whales usually live?" David asked.

"Most of them get to be at least twenty-five years old. They don't have any natural enemies—except people, that is."

"Hmm." David smiled, picturing Hound Dog being led like a puppy on a string—a *big* puppy. Giant, puppy-like dolphins didn't sound so bad, even though they ate seals.

He went back to hoping the whales would swim closer to the ferry.

But they never surfaced again, at least not that David could see. The rest of the trip was boring. He was glad when the ferry finally docked.

They got to their motel in Campbell River at about five o'clock. They always rented a room with a little kitchen so they could cook their own food. David snacked on a bacon and tomato sandwich while his grandfather sliced the sausage into a skillet.

"What time are we going to start out tomorrow?" David asked, brushing a tomato seed off the front of his shirt. The smell of the cooking sausage was making his mouth water.

"Let's shoot for five-thirty. The best time for fishing is always early in the morning and then again in the evening."

David groaned. "I hate getting up that early. But I'd rather get up to fish than to go to school!"

"Why doesn't that surprise me?" Mr. Ryckman murmured.

By sunrise the next morning, they were already heading out in their rented boat. David huddled inside his jacket, enjoying the salty smell of the air. They were going to spend the morning fishing around some of the smaller islands in the area.

David yawned, looking around. In the distance, the red-and-white Cape Mudge lighthouse jutted up from the rocks. Just below it, the lightkeeper's cottage looked like a dollhouse.

Mr. Ryckman slowed the boat and then turned it off. "Let's try mooching for a while, eh?" he suggested. Mooching is fishing while the boat drifts along with the current. "Maybe we can catch some salmon for lunch."

David was already opening his tackle box. "Sounds good to me. Getting up early always makes me hungry."

By late morning, though, David still hadn't caught much. His grandfather had already caught three salmon.

"Well," said Mr. Ryckman, enjoying himself, "I guess we've still got room for that six-foot salmon you were going to catch. But you'd better hurry. It's almost time for lunch."

David grinned sheepishly. "Let's talk about something else. When are you going to take me out to your gold claim so I can find lots of gold?"

"Oh, pretty soon, I imagine. Only we won't be hunting gold, remember. We'll just measure out the claim and clear away bushes. It will be very hard work."

David tugged gently on his line. Nothing. "It couldn't be any harder than learning stupid old French. Or trying to catch fish that don't want to be caught."

"You might be surprised. Just wait until you're out in the middle of nowhere someday, having to kick and claw your way across a steep mountainside. You might start wishing you were back in French class."

"No way," David said with confidence. He reeled in his line, then cast it toward a fishier-looking spot. "I can handle it."

/ / /

Sunday night, they both returned home with sunburns, dirty clothes, and a cooler full of salmon. Mrs. Ryckman greeted them with hugs.

"Phew, you smell like fish," she said, wrinkling her nose. "I guess that's a good sign, eh?"

"Sure," said Mr. Ryckman. He nudged David with his elbow. "Even David here finally managed to catch a fish or two."

"Hey!" David exclaimed. "Didn't I end up catching more than you?"

"I don't remember. I stopped counting after the first twenty or so."

David rolled his eyes. "Right, Oopa."

Mrs. Ryckman laughed. "Save your fish stories for later. I've got dinner waiting on the table."

Training for the Gold Claim

Over the next few weeks, David kept nagging his grandfather about taking him to the gold claim. Finally, Mr. Ryckman decided to take David on a day-long training hike nearby. He wanted to make sure the teenager could handle a hard mountain hike before taking him any farther out into the wilderness.

David didn't know about the plan until he walked in from school one Tuesday afternoon in late July. He found his grandfather playing with a new set of walkie-talkies.

"Where'd you get those, Oopa?" he asked, sending his French book sailing over onto the kitchen table. He wished he could send it out the window.

"Oh, I just picked them up at Radio Shack. Since it is such a beautiful day, I thought we might try them out this afternoon. Do you feel up to going on a hike?"

"Sure!" David exclaimed. "Where will we go?"

"I was thinking we could drive up to Cypress Bowl and hike the Howe Sound Crest Trail. If we leave pretty soon, we should be able to get down to Lion's Bay by seven o'clock."

David was surprised. They had hiked parts of that trail before. But all the way to Lion's Bay in just six or seven hours? They would have to hike a lot faster than usual. But if his grandfather could do it, so could he.

"Sounds good to me," he said. "But how will we get back home from Lion's Bay?"

"Grandma will pick us up. That's why we need the walkie-talkies. We'll leave one with her and take one with us. She'll drive to Lion's Bay around six-thirty, and we can radio down to tell her exactly when to expect us."

Mrs. Ryckman smiled. "He's just using this as an excuse to buy himself a new toy, David. He's been wanting walkie-talkies for a long time."

David picked up one of the radios, pressed the "talk" button, and spoke into it: "Testing, testing, testing." Nothing happened. "It's not working," he complained.

"Could be because I haven't put the batteries in yet," Mr. Ryckman said. "Hand it here, eh?"

While his grandfather tested the walkie-talkies, David got out his backpack. He dropped in his water bottle, a couple of oranges to snack on, and his whistle. His grandfather always insisted that they take along whistles in case they got separated. Whistles could be heard over a long distance and, he claimed, had even been known to scare off bears.

Mr. Ryckman added another water bottle, a small first-aid kit, the walkie-talkie, and a coiled rope to David's pack. "Rope can come in handy in the wilderness," he said. "Remember all the knots we practiced back when you were in Boy Scouts?"

"Sort of."

"Knowing how to tie a good knot can mean the difference between life and death."

David sighed; his grandfather was using his "teacher" voice again.

Mr. Ryckman continued, "Take a bowline, for instance. Let's say a friend of yours is stuck down in a hole, and you've got to get him up. You put a rope around him and tie it right, and you can pull him up just fine. Tie it wrong, and the knot will slip and cut him in half!"

David asked pointedly, "Didn't I already get this whole knot lecture as a Boy Scout, Oopa?"

Mr. Ryckman laughed. "Probably so." He pulled on his favorite hiking hat, a battered white "Gilligan" hat with drooping edges. "Well, sport, are you ready to tackle the wilderness? Grandma said she'd drop us off up at the trailhead."

The Howe Sound Crest Trail was a steep, rocky trail that stretched over nine miles [29 kilometers]. It started at Cypress Park and led through the mountains along the coast, the same mountain range David had seen from the ferry. The trail was only safe to hike in the summer months. In the winter there were a lot of avalanches.

At Cypress Park, David got out and drew a deep breath. The sky was a bright blue, the air cool and scented with pine. "This is a perfect day for a hike," he said happily.

Mr. Ryckman nodded. "It doesn't get much better than this." He glanced at his watch. "Well, it's almost one o'clock now. We'll have to hurry if we're going to get down to Lion's Bay by seven. Ready?"

"Sure!" David said. "Bye, Grandma. See you tonight!"

"Bye!" she replied. "You two be careful, now! I'll be listening for you on the walkie-talkie."

David waved and then fell in step beside his grandfather. He liked the springy, crunchy feel of the pine needles under his tennis shoes. It was like walking on a thick carpet.

Mr. Ryckman paused to push a button on his stopwatch. "I'm going to time our hike today," he said. "This isn't going to be an easy stroll. I want to see how tough you are before I decide whether to take you out to the gold claim."

David grinned. "No problem. I'm as tough as they come."

The first part of the trail led over Mount Strachan. They were crunching up the path side by side when

Mr. Ryckman paused again to pick up a long stick. He held it up and tested its weight.

"Looks like a good ginty stick," he said, stripping off the leaves and twigs to make it smooth. "Ginty" is a game in Ireland something like hockey. Mr. Ryckman always called his walking sticks ginty sticks. "I was watching for one."

The main trail was marked with small orange flags or sometimes orange paint splashed on rocks. It led along the side of the mountains facing the ocean.

They climbed Mount Strachan and then hiked back down to Strachan Meadows. A small orange sign there read You've Come 2.64 Kilometers.

Mr. Ryckman pulled out his stopwatch and pressed the button. "Forty-five minutes," he said with satisfaction. "We made good time on that stretch, but we should stop here to fill our water bottles at the creek. We might not find any more fresh water for hours."

David dug both bottles out of his backpack and tossed one to his grandfather. Then he knelt down and dunked his into the bubbling creek. The water was icy cold, even in July. By the time the bottle was full, his fingers felt frozen.

Mr. Ryckman stood up and stretched. "Well, Mount Strachan was easy, kind of a warm-up stroll. Now comes St. Marks."

David glanced up at the next slope. "No problem. I'm ready whenever you are."

Mr. Ryckman marked the time with his stopwatch. "OK, then. Let's get moving!"

The trail leading up St. Marks was rocky and a lot steeper. After almost an hour of climbing—*fast* climbing—they had still not reached the top.

"How are you doing?" Mr. Ryckman asked, puffing a little as he leaned forward on his walking stick.

"Fine," David replied. He was puffing a little too, but he tried to hide it. Taking the trail this fast made it seem a lot harder. Suddenly, the six or seven miles ahead seemed like a long way.

It took them an hour and ten minutes to make it all the way to the top of St. Marks. There was another sign waiting for them there: You Have Come 5.48 Kilometers.

David shook his head. The first two and a half kilometers to Strachan Meadows had only taken forty-five minutes. But it went a lot slower when it was all uphill!

It was going to be a long, long way to Lion's Bay.

On to Mount Unnecessary

Mr. Ryckman allowed only a short rest, and then it was back to the trail. They were hiking down the far side of St. Marks when they heard sounds coming from somewhere ahead. An older couple appeared on the trail below.

"Hi, there!" they called when they spotted David and Mr. Ryckman. "Nice day, eh?"

Mr. Ryckman nodded. "Sure is." As the couple passed by, David gave them a friendly wave. He was glad to be on the way down instead of up!

"You don't see too many people back in here during the week," Mr. Ryckman said as they continued down the trail. "We've pretty much got the whole place to ourselves."

He was thumping his walking stick on the ground with each step. *Thump, thump, thump.* Between that and his Gilligan's Island hat, he looked pretty funny. David was suddenly glad there weren't more people around to see them.

At the bottom of St. Marks, Mr. Ryckman nodded toward the next mountain. It had two small peaks, like devils' horns. "We'll climb Mount Unnecessary next, and then follow the ridge all the way over to West Lion Mountain. I told Grandma I'd try to call her from the top of West Lion."

Mr. Ryckman shaded his eyes for a moment to study the mountain in the distance. The sun was shin- ing and the sky was clear blue, but a hazy cloud seemed to be gathering over West Lion's rocky peak.

He frowned. "Unless that cloud moves on pretty quick, we might have to skip West Lion and go straight down to Lion's Bay," he said. "It's not safe up here when bad weather moves in. When these rocks get wet, they're as slippery as ice." He checked his stopwatch. "Well, on to Mount Unnecessary!"

David stretched. "I bet Mount Unnecessary was named by some poor hiker sick of climbing."

Mr. Ryckman raised one bushy eyebrow. "Getting tired already?"

David caught the meaning behind his words. He was testing him! "No way. Come on, I'll race you to the top!"

The trail up Mount Unnecessary was even steeper and narrower than the last one. They had to scramble over rocks and fallen logs and push their way past thick branches. It was a workout, especially going so fast.

Mr. Ryckman paused once when he spotted a narrow, overgrown trail branching off to their left.

"I think that's the old trail down to Lion's Bay," he said. "I used to hike it years ago when it was the *only* trail. If I remember right, it runs about five hundred feet lower than the new trail." He looked over at David. "Still doing OK? We've been moving pretty fast."

"I feel great!" David said. "Why don't we jog the rest of the way?" If his grandfather was trying to test him, he might as well make it sound good.

Mr. Ryckman laughed. "You're a pretty tough young lad. I thought for sure you'd be griping by now. I'm impressed!"

David tried to hide his pleasure. It wasn't easy to impress his grandfather.

By the time they reached the top of Mount Unnecessary's first peak, it was four-thirty. They stopped to rest and look around. Now that they were up above the trees, they had a clear view of the ocean on their left. At times they could see the B. C. ferry chugging along far below, looking like a little bathtub toy.

Mr. Ryckman drank some water and leaned back against a rock. "We don't have that much farther to go now. Just over the north peak and then along Unnecessary Ridge. We're going to skip West Lion this time." The cloud over the mountain's peak still hadn't budged. If anything, it was bigger—and darker.

David sat on a boulder and peeled an orange. The sun was still warm, but the wind was cool. He was glad he was wearing a jacket over his thin T-shirt.

When they got started again, it only took them about thirty minutes to climb the north peak. Near the top, David noticed a few wisps of fog drifting past. At almost the same moment, a dark shadow passed over the sun. He glanced up to see a cloud moving in overhead.

"We'd better get moving," Mr. Ryckman said. "It almost never storms in the middle of July, but I don't want to take any chances. I guess I should have paid more attention to that cloud over West Lion. It looks like it's spreading."

They hurried along the ridge, watching for the trail down to Lion's Bay. Although Unnecessary Ridge was fairly flat, it was narrow with steep drop-offs on both sides. In damp weather it would be easy to slip on the rocks.

But within minutes the fog closed in around them. It was as if they had suddenly walked into the middle of a thick white cloud. Mr. Ryckman wasn't happy.

"We've got a problem, David," he said. "I don't like having you on this ridge in a fog. Let's just sit down and wait for a while to see if it lifts, eh?" He added, "You're probably about ready for a rest anyway."

David shrugged. He didn't want to admit it, but he *was* tired. They had walked over four miles since lunchtime, most of it uphill. His legs and ankles were starting to ache. He sat down and stretched out on the rocky ground, using his backpack for a pillow.

Mr. Ryckman smiled. He stretched out a few feet away from David. "Think I'll take a little nap while we wait." He scooted his Gilligan hat forward to cover his face.

David stared up at the fog, watching it swirl and dance through the air above him. He wasn't a bit sleepy.

"Oopa?" he said.

"I'm asleep," came his grandfather's gruff reply.

"No, you're not."

Mr. Ryckman slowly sat up and slid his hat back onto the top of his head. "OK, so I'm not. What do you want?"

"Nothing. I'm just bored."

Mr. Ryckman shook his head in mock disbelief. "You wake me up from a sound sleep for nothing? I ought to throw you off the mountain!" He glanced around at the thick white haze before adding solemnly, "It looks like a good day for dying."

David laughed. The line was a quote from one of his favorite movies, *Little Big Man*. In it, an old Indian chief keeps planning his own death with no great success.

Mr. Ryckman slowly stretched back out on the ground, arms stiff to his sides, eyes closed. David waited, knowing what was coming next. After a minute or two, his grandfather opened one eye. "Am I dead yet?" he asked.

"Sorry, Oopa. It didn't work this time. You're still here with me."

Mr. Ryckman made a face. "I was afraid of that. Oh well, if I'm not going to die I guess I'd better get up. These rocks aren't exactly soft."

A Slippery Slope

They waited for another twenty or thirty minutes, but the fog stayed as thick as ever. Finally, Mr. Ryckman sighed. "Well, I can't take you down the trail to Lion's Bay in this. It's way too steep and slippery." He glanced at his watch. "Plus, it's almost six-thirty. If we go all the way back along the main trail, it'll be dark before we get there."

"And we don't have flashlights," David pointed out. "Besides, Grandma will be waiting for us in Lion's Bay."

Mr. Ryckman tapped his walking stick on the ground, thinking. "We might try using the old trail down to Lion's Bay. It's lower, so it might be below the fog. It used to be a pretty good trail."

David liked the idea of taking a trail not everybody knew about. It sounded a little more adventurous.

"Sounds good to me. I'd rather do that than go all the way back."

"Then let's go. I'll radio Grandma in a few minutes to let her know we might be late."

Moving carefully, they made their way back along the ridge. The fog made it hard to see, even though the trail was clearly marked. It took them almost an hour to get back to the old trail.

"Before we start down, let's call Grandma," Mr. Ryckman said. "I don't want her to worry. You know what she's like."

"Yeah." David dug the walkie-talkie out of his backpack. Mr. Ryckman pulled the antenna up and pressed the "talk" button. "Margaret? Can you hear me?"

David listened intently. The radio made some loud crackling sounds but nothing that sounded like his grandmother.

"Better try again, Oopa," he said.

Mr. Ryckman spoke into the walkie-talkie again, louder this time. "Margaret! Helloooo, Margaret! This is Bud. Answer if you can hear me."

Nothing. He finally pushed the antenna down. "All these boulders are probably blocking our reception. We'll try again in a few minutes. If I remember right, there's a big clearing and an old logging road not too far down this trail."

David followed as his grandfather led off down the narrow, overgrown path. He was cheered by the thought that they would soon be out of the fog. He hated not being able to see. It was kind of creepy.

The trail started off on a gentle slope but quickly became steep. Mr. Ryckman was surprised.

"I don't remember it being like this," he said, leaning on his stick as he edged down a sharp drop. "But we should be hitting the clearing soon. Once we get there, it'll be easy. Just be careful not to slip."

David didn't like taking it slow. He liked to scramble down the slopes at a trot, sending loose pebbles flying in every direction. Kind of like skiing without skis—or snow!

"David!" Mr. Ryckman scolded. "You can't go skipping around on a mountain in fog like this. Slow down!"

"Sorry, Oopa," David said. "It's easier for me to go fast."

The trail gradually got steeper and steeper. Several times they had to grab onto rocks or tree limbs to keep from slipping. On the worst parts, Mr. Ryckman insisted on climbing down first. The fog stayed as thick as ever.

Every ten minutes Mr. Ryckman tried the walkie-talkie again. "Margaret!" he yelled, as if that would help the radio waves go farther. "Margaret, it's Bud!" There was never an answer. By eight o'clock, he was looking worried.

"I told Grandma to expect us by six-thirty or seven," he said. "I wish I could get through to her."

Huddled in the damp fog, David suddenly shivered and pulled his jacket closer. "How much farther is it to Lion's Bay?"

"Not too far. Maybe another mile." Mr. Ryckman peered through the fog in frustration. "The clearing can't be much farther now."

But soon after that, they came to the worst part of the trail yet—a steep slope covered with loose rocks. And if that weren't enough, there was a fifty-story drop just below. If they started sliding, they could go right over the edge!

Mr. Ryckman looked grim. If the mountainside above them hadn't been so steep, he might have been tempted to turn around. But now they had no choice. They had to keep going.

He studied the area below them carefully. Bushes and small fir trees were growing out from between the rocks and boulders. They should make good handholds.

"Well," he said, "where there's a will, there's a way! I'll check it out first and see how bad it is. Stay up here until I call you. Keep the rope handy just in case."

David nodded. He watched as his grandfather eased his way down the slope, grabbing onto the small trees and bushes. It took him almost fifteen minutes to get to the more level area on the trail below.

"OK!" he called up to David. "You can start down now, but be very, very careful."

"Righto!" David shouted back.

After his first few steps, however, the teenager grew impatient. He sat down and started sliding down toward his grandfather, digging his tennis shoes into the rocks to slow himself down. Fifteen seconds later he skidded to a halt at the bottom. He jumped up, panting and grinning. "Hi, Oopa!" he said cheerfully.

Mr. Ryckman was angry. "David!" he snapped. "Use your brains, will you? What do you think this is, a game?"

"Um, no, sir," he stammered. "I just—"

"This is no place for foolishness!" Mr. Ryckman pointed to the long drop just below them. "What if you'd kept sliding? You'd have gone off before I could stop you!"

David started to say, "But I didn't!" and then thought better of it. "I'm sorry, Oopa. I didn't mean to scare you."

Mr. Ryckman suddenly looked tired. "All right, all right. Come on, then. Let's see if we can get out of here."

Turning to lead off down the trail, Mr. Ryckman stepped on a loose pebble. Without warning, his feet shot out from under him. He fell backward onto the rocks, hitting his head with a sharp *crack!* Dazed, he tumbled sideways and started sliding, headfirst, down toward the drop.

"Oopa!" David screamed. "Oopa, watch out!" He watched, horrified, as his grandfather clawed at the rocks, trying to stop.

At the last second Mr. Ryckman grabbed desperately at a small fir tree, but it uprooted in his hand. With a terrified scream, he disappeared over the edge.

A Courageous Climb

David stood frozen in place, unable to believe what had just happened. He could hear his grandfather's body crashing and banging down the mountainside. A shower of rocks and pebbles were falling with him. The sounds seemed to go on for a long time.

Finally, there was silence. David took a shaky breath that turned into a deep sob. "Oopa!" he cried. "*Oopa!* Are you all right?"

There was no reply. Forgetting all his grandfather's warnings, David scrambled down to peer over the edge. What he saw made him gasp. Far, far below, half hidden by the fog, his grandfather's limp body was bent backwards over a huge boulder.

"Oopa!" he shouted. "Answer me! Are you all right?"

His grandfather didn't move, but David thought he heard a faint moan. "Oopa, can you hear me? Tell me if you're alive!" His voice was now pleading. He couldn't be dead. He couldn't!

There was no answer. David made a decision. "I'm coming down there!" he yelled. "I'm coming, Oopa. Just hold on!"

Breathing hard, the teenager flattened out onto his stomach and slid one leg over the edge. He tried not to think about what would happen if he fell too.

It looked impossible, but *where there's a will, there's a way*, he told himself. It was one of his grandfather's favorite sayings.

Then he remembered his backpack. What if it made him lose his balance? He took it off and flung it down the slope, watching it hit and bounce off the rocks all the way down. That was probably what his grandfather's body had done. The thought made David feel sick.

It was time to start climbing.

He dangled both legs over the edge, digging into the rocks with the toes of his tennis shoes. His heart was beating so hard that it pounded in his ears like a drum. He stretched his left foot down, found a toehold, and then slid his right hand down to grasp the corner of a rock. He knew he should take it slow, but his grandfather might be dying. He had to hurry!

Where there's a will, there's a way.

Left foot. Right hand. Right foot. Left hand. David scrambled down as fast as he could, grabbing rocks and bushes. Every second counted if his grandfather was going to survive. He tried not to picture the rocks far below. He didn't feel the dampness of the fog, or the coldness of the boulders under his hands. All his thoughts were focused on keeping his grip with his fingertips and toes.

Within minutes, his hands were torn and bleeding, his fingernails jammed with sharp gravel. Twice, rocks crumbled under his feet, leaving him clawing to keep his grip. David listened as they bounced and clattered down the slope. He was afraid they might hit his grandfather, but there wasn't anything he could do about it. He had to keep going.

Ten endless minutes later, he was almost to the bottom. "I'm coming, Oopa!" he said.

Then, unbelievably, he was standing on level ground again. Heart pounding, David hurried over to his grandfather's side. The sight of his injuries made him gasp.

Mr. Ryckman's forehead was deeply gashed, his flesh split open almost from ear to ear. He was so covered with blood and dirt that it took David a moment to realize that most of his clothes had been ripped off. All that was left were his underwear and shoes—and they were drenched in blood.

David stared at him. Was he dead? He couldn't tell. He leaned close to his ear. "Oopa, can you hear me? It's David!"

Mr. Ryckman didn't answer, but David thought he could see his chest moving. At least he was still breathing! He looked around wildly, wondering what he should do next. If only he could remember all Oopa's first aid lectures! He'd never thought he would need to know all that stuff. He wished he had listened better.

Stop the bleeding. Wasn't that one of the first things you were supposed to do?

"OK, Oopa," he said shakily, "I'm going to try to stop your bleeding." The deep cut on his forehead looked the worst. David gently pushed the flaps of torn skin back in place and then wrapped his jacket around Oopa's head like a bandage. To keep it tight, he tied the jacket sleeves together in the front. He knew pressure was supposed to stop bleeding, so he tugged the sleeves tighter, hoping it would help.

Then he remembered that unconscious people sometimes choke on their own tongues. Carefully, afraid he would hurt him even more, David rolled his grandfather over onto his side. There were other deep gashes all over his body. David's hands came away red with blood. He hastily wiped them off on the boulder.

Now what? David suddenly remembered the walkie-talkie. He fumbled it out of his backpack, hoping it wasn't smashed. It was full of dirt and dented in several places from being thrown down the slope, but it might still work. He slid up the antenna and pressed the Talk button.

"Mayday, mayday!" he said. He wasn't sure if that was the correct call for help on the radio, so he added, "Emergency! This is an emergency! Can anyone hear me?"

He released the button and waited. The only answer was static. He tried a few more times before shoving the radio back into his pack. What should he do now?

His grandfather had landed off to one side of a wide, and mostly dry, creekbed. Should they just wait here for help? But they had left the main trail. Nobody would know where to look.

David glanced over at his grandfather. The jacket had slipped off his head, and the gash was bleeding again. He tied it back on the best he could. His grandfather's face was gray now, and it didn't look like he was breathing anymore. David wondered with a sinking heart if he had broken his neck when he fell.

But if he *was* still alive, he wouldn't last long. He needed help, and he needed it fast!

"I'm going to get help, Oopa," he said, fighting back tears. "You just wait here, and don't move. Do you hear me? I'm going to get help!"

Mr. Ryckman didn't answer. David grabbed his backpack and started to run, following the creek down the mountain toward the ocean.

Alone on the Mountain

Running as fast as he could, the teenager leaped over rocks and splashed through the shallow creek. He quickly decided it must be Newman's Creek, which crossed the highway below. If he followed it all the way down, maybe he could stop a car.

As the creek snaked down the mountainside, though, it grew narrower and deeper. Soon it plunged down in small waterfalls. David recklessly jumped down most of the steep drops, but several times he had to climb down and wade through waist-deep water. In his thin pants and T-shirt, he was soon soaked and shivering. The fog was still everywhere, and now the sun was going down. He kept running, trying not to think about being cold.

He had run for almost half an hour when the creekbed abruptly ended in a sheer waterfall. The water tumbled straight down into a deep, cloud-filled ravine. The ravine curved away out of sight on both sides, like a huge horseshoe.

Panting, David tried to figure out what to do. Somehow, he had to cross the ravine to get down to the highway.

He saw a small rock ledge sticking out about fifty feet below and for one wild moment thought about jumping for it. He then realized how stupid that would be. If he fell and broke his neck, nobody would ever find his grandfather. He had to find another way.

Climbing out of the creekbed, David hurried along the edge of the ravine, looking for a way down. Finally, through a narrow rock opening, he saw what looked like a good path. It seemed to slope down toward a more level area below.

But like the trail down to Lion's Bay, its looks were deceptive. Almost immediately, David found himself on a crumbling slope too steep to stand on. With each movement, rocks broke off and slid down into the ravine. He now saw that, instead of leading down to the area he'd hoped, the path led straight to the edge of a cliff.

Another dead end.

He quickly turned around. But when he tried to climb back up, the crumbling rock kept breaking loose, sending him sliding backward. The harder he tried, the more he slid. There was nothing to hold on to, no way to pull himself up.

Finally he sat still, trying to think. What now? What could he do? He was stuck with nowhere to go.

Worst of all, while he sat there, helpless, his grandfather was slowly bleeding to death—if he wasn't dead already. David thought of his still, gray face and broken body. "I'm sorry, Oopa," he said with a sob. "I'm sorry!"

/ / /

Numb with misery, David huddled in the deepening gloom. As night approached, the temperature dropped. The cold wind felt like a knife when it hit his wet clothes. He couldn't stop shivering.

Then he remembered the walkie-talkie. If only it would work, just once, he might get through to someone who could send help. Where there's a will, there's a way, he told himself again. He suddenly felt more hopeful.

But first he needed to find a safer spot to sit. Right now, even the smallest movement made him slide. He was afraid that if he tried to take off his backpack, he might go flying over the edge. David strained his eyes down the slope. If he couldn't go up, he would have to go down.

Just below him were two baby fir trees, growing side by side. They were perched right on the cliff's edge. The biggest one had a trunk about the size of the thick end of a baseball bat, the smallest like a broom handle. If he could slide down to them, maybe he could brace his feet against them.

Of course if he missed, he would go off the cliff. That was a chance he decided he would have to take.

Taking a deep breath, David leaned forward and scooted, like he was starting down a slide. Once he started moving, he slid faster and faster. He tried to line his feet up with the little trees. He just hoped they wouldn't bend or break.

His tennis shoes hit both trees at the same time. The smaller one bent, but the bigger one stood firm. It stopped him less than a foot from the edge. David felt almost sick with relief, knowing how close he had come to falling off the cliff!

He quickly pulled out the walkie-talkie, keeping a good grip on his backpack so it wouldn't slide off. "Mayday! Mayday! Emergency!" he yelled. "Can anybody hear me?"

Please, he prayed, straining his ears for a reply. *Please let it work this time!*

After a few seconds, a faint voice drifted back to him: "I can hear you. Who is this?" It sounded like a woman.

The teenager let out his breath in a gasp. He hadn't really expected an answer. He suddenly felt both excited and panicked. What if the woman disappeared before he could tell her about his grandfather?

"My name's David James!" he yelled. "I need help! I'm stuck on a mountain! I think my grandfather's dead!"

A long moment passed. "Is this a joke?"

"No!" David shouted. "This is not a joke! Call my parents! Please!"

The woman must have heard the desperation in his voice. "Give me your parents' phone number."

David was breathing as hard as if he'd been running. He yelled the number and then added, "Please tell them to hurry!"

"I'll call right now," the woman told him.

With trembling hands, David held the walkie-talkie close to his chest. He couldn't drop it now. It was his only link to the outside world.

Several minutes later, a man's voice came over the radio, his voice distant. "David? I've got your parents on the line. I'm going to try to put you through to them now."

David held his breath. Could they do that with a walkie-talkie?

"David! Are you all right?" It was his father, but David could hardly make out his words.

"I'm OK," he shouted back, "but there's been a terrible accident. I don't think Oopa made it!"

There was a long pause. He held the walkie-talkie up to his ear. It couldn't cut off now. He had to tell them where he was!

"Hi, honey." It was his mother's voice this time. "I just ran next door and called Search and Rescue. Dad and I are leaving right now to come to Cypress Bowl. Can you hear me?"

"Yes!" David said, almost crying with relief. "Listen, Oopa is up in a dry creekbed . . . I think it's Newman's Creek. I'm further down, on the edge of a ravine." He swallowed hard. "I love you, Mum."

"I love you too. We're on our way. Everything's going to be OK."

After his mother hung up, David talked to the man for a few more minutes until the signal faded. Then there was nothing left but static. Once again, he was alone on the cold, foggy mountainside.

Losing Hope

Darkness fell. The air grew even colder. David tried to distract himself by looking around, but there wasn't much to see. The thick fog blotted out everything around him. Far off to his left, he thought he saw some lights twinkling, but he didn't know what they were. Could they be stars? They seemed awfully low. As time dragged on he grew discouraged. By now, his grandfather was almost surely dead. On top of his injuries, almost all of his clothes had been torn off when he fell. He could never survive in this cold.

Grandma's going to be so sad, David thought hopelessly. Her heart will probably break, and then she'll die too. The thought of losing both of them at once was too much. Tears started running down his face, making him feel even colder.

"Please, Lord," he whispered through chattering teeth. "Please let Oopa somehow be all right. Let us live through this. We need help!"

It was almost eleven o'clock when a deep, cheerful voice suddenly boomed from the walkie-talkie. "Hello, hello. Can you hear me?"

David was fumbling with his half-frozen hands to pick it up when another man spoke: "Yes, yes, yes! I can hear you!"

Finally, David got his finger on the "talk" button. He didn't wait to be polite. "Mayday!" he yelled. "Emergency! I need help!"

The first man answered right away. "What's wrong? Who is this?"

"My name's David James. I was hiking with my grandfather, and he fell and got hurt. I was trying to get help for him, but I got stuck. I think he's dead."

There was a short pause. "All right, David. My name is Michael, and I'm down here in Horseshoe Bay. I'll call the police right now. Don't you worry about a thing, guy."

David waited, praying this voice wouldn't fade away like the last one. It really helped to have somebody to talk to, even if they were miles away.

Soon Michael returned to the radio. "I have good news," he said. "The police already have two Search and Rescue teams out looking for you. They said your mom called them about an hour ago."

David was relieved. "That's good. But how are they going to find me? It's really dark and foggy up here."

"When I told them I was talking to you, they said they'd come here to Horseshoe Bay to set up. They said for you to listen for the search team. They've got flashlights and whistles."

Whistles! David had forgotten all about his. "I have a whistle in my backpack!" he said.

"Then start blowing it every few minutes, eh? That'll help them find you a lot quicker."

David dug out the whistle, glad to have something useful to do. He blew it again and again, as loud as he could, but there were no answering whistles from the dark mountains around him.

By eleven-thirty, his excitement was wearing off. He started shivering again. "Michael?" he said. "Are you sure they're coming? I don't hear anybody."

"Just be patient, guy. It takes time."

David hesitated. "Listen, can you put me through to my house? Another guy did that so I could talk to my parents."

"I'll give it a try. Maybe I can hold the walkie-talkie up to the phone. I just bought these walkie-talkies this afternoon, so I don't know too much about them. I was testing them for the first time when I heard you."

Michael called David's house and then held the walkie-talkie up to the phone so he could talk to Jennifer, his fourteen-year-old sister.

"How's everybody doing?" David asked. He had nothing important to say, but he felt better talking to his family. It helped take his mind off the cold.

"We're OK. Mum and Dad are on their way to Cypress Bowl. Are you OK?"

"Sort of . . ." David swallowed hard, thinking of his grandfather. "Can you put Brian and Mark on?" Brian and Mark were his seven-year-old twin brothers. He talked to them for a few minutes and then to his other sister, twelve-year-old Kathleen.

Finally, David ran out of things to say. "Well, I love all of you," he said. "I guess I'll talk to you later." He usually didn't say stuff like that to his little brothers and sisters, but somehow it seemed important now. After they hung up, he felt more lonely than ever.

It was almost midnight. What was taking the rescuers so long? If they didn't get there soon, he was going to freeze. He thought again of his grandfather, and a lump rose in his throat. Why had this happened?

"David?" Michael checked on him whenever he got quiet. "How're you doing up there?"

"T-t-terrible," David said through chattering teeth. "I'm freezing to death."

"It won't be long now. They'll get you out of there, you'll see."

"Have they found my grandfather yet?"

"I'm afraid not. But they won't give up until they do."

David was too miserable to be nice. "I hope they make it while I'm still alive."

"Hey, now, don't you talk like that!" Michael said sharply. "You just keep blowing that whistle."

"OK." David pulled out the whistle and blew it again but, as usual, there was no reply.

Around midnight, Mr. and Mrs. James arrived at Horseshoe Bay. They used Michael's walkie-talkie to talk to David.

"Hi, honey. It's Mum." His mother's voice sounded strained. "Are you all right?"

"I'm OK. But Mum . . . I think Oopa's dead." He hadn't really meant to blurt it out like that, but he didn't know how else to tell her. She needed to know. After all, Oopa was her father.

"We'll have to deal with that later," Mrs. James said firmly. "Right now let's just take one thing at a time."

"OK." Somehow, just knowing his parents were down there made him feel better. He knew they wouldn't give up on him, no matter what.

Over the next few hours, David talked back and forth with his mom and Michael. His mom tried to cheer him up by joking about ways he could keep warm.

"Try thinking warm thoughts," she suggested. "Think about fire and hot chocolate and vegetable soup."

David tried to play along. "I hate vegetable soup. I'll think about chicken soup instead."

But by three o'clock in the morning, the teenager was beginning to despair. Where were the searchers? He had blown his whistle until he had no air in him to blow, but the mountains around him stayed silent. What if he fell asleep? He could slip right off the edge! Or he might drop the walkie-talkie. His fingers were numb from the cold.

The Search Grows Desperate

Down in Horseshoe Bay, Mr. and Mrs. James were also getting frustrated. Finally, the search master came up with an idea. He used Michael's walkie-talkie to talk to David.

"From your description, we think you're facing the ocean," he said. "The lights you see off to your left are probably the lights here in Horseshoe Bay. We're going to get the B. C. ferry to cruise along the coast, shining a big spotlight up onto the mountains. As soon as it hits you, yell into your walkie-talkie. If we can pinpoint your general location it might speed things up."

"Good idea!" David said. Anything would be better than sitting there, half frozen, in the dark. He had forgotten what it felt like to be warm.

About twenty minutes later, the thick fog in front of him suddenly lit up. "I see the spotlight!" he shouted excitedly. "It's right on me!"

But the light was already sweeping off to his right. By the time Search and Rescue passed David's message on to the ferry, it was already far away.

The ferry tried again, but the same thing happened. After several more tries, they finally gave up. They couldn't stop in time to keep the light pointing at David.

Still, at least Search and Rescue had a better idea now of where to look for him. "Don't give up, honey," Mrs. James said. "They're going all through the woods, calling and blowing whistles. Can you hear anything?"

"No," David said shortly. He had been so excited when he'd seen the spotlight. He had thought it was all almost over. Now he found himself fighting back tears again.

Please make them hurry, he prayed. He was so cold now that he hurt all over. And as he thought about his grandfather lying all alone in the dry, rocky creekbed, the hurt inside him was much, much worse. He wondered if the accident had been his fault. Oopa had just been scolding him about not being careful. Had that distracted him?

"Please," he sobbed aloud. "Please, Lord, let Oopa be alive. I love him so much."

Suddenly, he heard a faint whistle. David thought at first that he might be imagining it. But when he heard it again, he gasped. The search team!

He grabbed his own whistle and blew it long and loud. Then he listened again, wanting to make sure. After a moment a long, loud whistle came in reply. They had heard him!

"Over here!" he shouted. "I'm over here!" His grandfather always said that whistles carried a lot farther than voices, but he couldn't help shouting. At last!

But the promising moment soon turned into another near miss. The jumbled rocks made it impossible for the searchers to tell which way his whistle was coming from. They still couldn't find him!

Four o'clock and then four-thirty came. David was so cold and tired that he couldn't think straight. He felt like a frozen statue, unable to move. Even if they found him now, he couldn't stand up. How would they get him down?

About five o'clock the sky started getting lighter. But even as the sun rose, the fog kept David from seeing much of anything. Numb from the cold and half asleep, he let his mind wander. He thought about Oopa . . . the gold claim they would never visit now . . . his little brothers and sisters . . . French class . . .

French class! David sat up. He was going to miss French this morning! It would be his second absence. He would fail! Then he realized what a stupid thing that was to be worrying about. His grandfather was dead and he was lost. Who cared if he failed French?

Just then the walkie-talkie crackled. "David!" his mother said. "We just heard that a helicopter is coming out to look for you."

"How will it see anything through this fog?"

"I don't know . . . maybe it will clear up soon."

After all the disappointments, David couldn't get too excited. What would happen if they couldn't see him? Would they call off the search until the fog lifted? It could be days!

The helicopter didn't start its search until after six. By then the batteries in the walkie-talkie were starting to run low. Mrs. James told David to save his batteries by not talking unless he had to.

"Listen carefully," she said. "They're going to fly the helicopter back and forth, going very slow. As soon as you see it, start giving directions about which way it should go. Just say up, down, right, or left. As soon as it's straight above you, yell!"

David waited impatiently. Every now and then there would be an opening in the fog, and he would catch a glimpse of the ocean. It was frustrating to be so close to everything—towns, highways, cars—and not be able to get there. But he knew that people had died in these mountains within sight of town.

It was almost six-thirty when David heard the faint thrum-thrum-thrum of a helicopter. A few minutes later, he spotted it. It was off to his left and too far down.

"Go up and right!" he shouted. "Up and right!" He hoped they could understand him. The last time he had tried to talk they said his voice was fading in and out.

But they must have heard at least part of it. The helicopter inched up and to the right.

"Up more!" he yelled. "More to the right!"

The helicopter didn't move. "David?" This time it was a man's voice. "Say it again, and space your words out. We can't understand you."

"UP . . . AND . . . RIGHT!" David screamed, praying they could hear him. If they got this close and missed him again, he didn't think he could take it.

Slowly, the helicopter edged toward him. Closer . . . closer . . .

"Stop!" he yelled. "They're right above me! Stop!" It was only then that he realized he was shouting into a dead walkie-talkie. He waved frantically, trying to get the pilot's attention. Had they heard him in time?

The pilot leaned out and waved.

David felt like crying and laughing all at the same time. He'd been found!

But What about Oopa?

After that, everything moved fast. A rescuer was lowered onto the mountainside next to David. He quickly strapped David into a harness and then motioned to the helicopter to pull them up. As he dangled high in the air above the ravine, David suddenly remembered his grandfather's knot lecture. He just hoped his rescuer knew how to tie a good bowline knot!

A moment later, he was inside the helicopter. It was an old war helicopter, with room inside for over twenty people. One of the crew members unstrapped him and then handed him a blanket.

"Th-th-thanks," David said, wrapping it around his shoulders. He had never felt anything nicer than that warm, thick blanket.

An ambulance was waiting for them down at Cypress Park. As a paramedic helped him onto a stretcher, David asked weakly, "Have they found my grandfather yet?"

"Not yet. But I think they're going to take the helicopter back up to look for him."

"I need to stay and help. I can show them exactly where he is!"

The paramedic shook his head. "You're going to Lion's Gate Hospital. You're not in any shape to go climbing mountains right now."

Just then, Mr. and Mrs. James arrived. After hugging and kissing David like he was a little kid, his mom said the same thing. "You're shivering all over. You're going straight to the hospital."

David argued all the way there, but no one would listen. He was certain by now that his grandfather was dead, but he couldn't stand the thought of him lying out there all alone. Why wouldn't anyone listen?

At Lion's Gate Hospital, the doctors found that David had a mild case of hypothermia; his body temperature was down to only 93 degrees. But with warm food and blankets, David was soon as good as new—almost. He couldn't relax until his grandfather was found. He had to get back to the mountain!

Finally, he talked his parents into taking him back to Cypress Park. Once there, he planted himself in front of the search master. "I can show you where my grandfather is," he said. "Let me go up in the helicopter with you!"

The search master looked down at him. "Well . . ." he said doubtfully, "the thing is, we're using a smaller helicopter now. It just holds three people: the pilot, a co-pilot, and a doctor. There isn't room for you."

David stuck out his jaw. "I'm telling you, I can take you straight to him. You might never find him otherwise."

The search master finally smiled. "Tell you what. Give us just a little while longer. If we don't find him in another hour or two, we'll make room for you to go along. Fair enough?"

David nodded unhappily. "I think he's already dead, but . . ."

"I know. We'll find him. Don't you worry."

David went to wait with his parents and grandmother in a small cafeteria nearby. Mrs. Ryckman was crying, her hands covering her face. David put his arm around her.

"I'm sorry, Grandma," he said helplessly. "I really tried my best to help Oopa. I didn't know what else to do."

Mrs. Ryckman hugged him tearfully. "I know you did, honey. I just wish they would find him!"

David pressed his lips together. He had waited long enough. They had to let him help! He stood up, planning to go find the search master again.

Just then a man burst into the room. "They've spotted Mr. Ryckman!" he shouted. "And they said it looks like he's moving! They're sending a team down after him now. They're going to take him to the trauma center at Vancouver General Hospital."

David hugged his grandmother, unable to believe it. He remembered all the times he had prayed for a miracle as he sat shivering in the dark. But unless he saw his grandfather with his own eyes, he wouldn't believe it. It wasn't possible!

The family raced to Vancouver General. An hour later Mr. Ryckman finally arrived. The doctor called Mrs. Ryckman and Mr. and Mrs. James in, leaving David sitting in the waiting room. But almost immediately, Mrs. James ran back in.

"David!" she said excitedly. "Oopa is alive! They're taking him in now to operate on him, but he's alive! They think he's going to be fine!"

David stared at her. "You're just telling me that, aren't you, Mum? Tell me the truth. I *saw* him. He's dead, isn't he?"

Mrs. James hesitated. "Wait right here."

A moment later a doctor appeared. "David? Come with me, please."

David followed him without saying a word. The doctor led him into a small room with a high bed. Mr. Ryckman was lying there with lots of tubes hooked to him.

As David stared, his grandfather turned his head and smiled. "Hi there, sport," he said weakly. "How you doing?"

"Oopa!" David could hardly talk. "I thought . . . I thought . . . "

"I heard they were having a hard time convincing you I was alive, so I told them to bring you in here to see for yourself." Mr. Ryckman chuckled. "You saved my life, you know. The doctor says I would've bled to death if it weren't for you."

The doctor gently tapped David's shoulder. "I need you to go back out with your parents now. We'll get your grandpa fixed up for you. Then you can talk to him again."

"Thanks," David said. He walked out slowly, feeling like he was in a dream. The impossible had happened. His grandfather was alive!

A lump rose in his throat. *Thank You,* he said silently.

/ / /

Mr. Ryckman was in surgery for over six hours. When he first arrived, his body temperature was down to 79 degrees. His forehead, chin, back, right arm, and right leg were all cut to the bone, and he also had dozens of other smaller cuts all over his body. It took hundreds of stitches to sew him back together.

He also had gravel jammed under all ten fingernails from clawing at the rocks on his way down. He even had several sharp pieces of rock jammed deep into his leg bones. The doctor had never seen anything like it.

"It's a miracle he survived after falling that far," he said. "If that boy hadn't gotten to him as fast as he did, he wouldn't have made it."

The search master said the same thing. "He should've died," he told Mrs. Ryckman. "We still can't figure out how David climbed down that slope. The search team couldn't have done it, and they're trained climbers!" They never found any trace of Mr. Ryckman's coat, gloves, shirt, sweater, or his Gilligan hat, but they did finally find his gold stopwatch. It was dangling from a bush hundreds of feet up the slope.

Over the next few weeks, David spent a lot of time at the hospital. His grandfather told him about a strange dream he'd had that night on the mountain.

"I dreamed we hiked all the way down to Lion's Bay, just like we planned," Mr. Ryckman recalled. "I watched you get into the car with your grandma. Then, for some reason, I hiked back up alone. When I woke up, I didn't know it was all a dream. I thought you were safe with Grandma." He shook his head. "If I'd known you were wandering around up there by yourself, I would've gone looking for you and gotten myself killed for sure."

David wondered about that. So many weird coincidences had led to their survival.

His grandfather, who had never used walkie-talkies on any of their other hikes, had suddenly decided to buy some for that trip. Why?

Michael, the man down in Horseshoe Bay, had also suddenly decided to buy walkie-talkies that same afternoon—exactly the same brand and model as Mr. Ryckman's!

David's walkie-talkie had lasted just long enough for the rescue helicopter to spot him. One second later and he could not have told them when to stop.

And what about his grandfather's odd dream? It had caused him to wait calmly for rescue instead of trying to hike with terrible injuries.

"Oopa?" David said thoughtfully. "Something kept bothering me while I was stuck up there. Right before you fell, you were yelling at me. I thought it might have been my fault that you fell off."

Mr. Ryckman shot David an amused glance. "Why, did you push me?" he demanded.

"No! I just thought I might have distracted you or something."

Mr. Ryckman reached over to ruffle David's hair. "Well, sport, I'll tell you what I think." He folded his arms across his chest like the old Indian chief in the movie. "I think it was a good day to die . . . but lucky for me, I had a grandson too tough to let it happen!"

David James was later awarded
the Canadian Medal of Bravery
for his help in Mr. Ryckman's rescue.

/ / /

David and Grandpa Bud Ryckman

MISSING

Raymond Lauriano
Age 11 Black hair, Brown eyes
Last seen Wednesday, 6/2
$2,000 Reward
If you have any information, call the El Monte
Police Department at (818) 580-2110

Flyer posted in El Monte, California,
during the search for Raymond Lauriano.

Kidnapped!

The Raymond Lauriano Story

"C'mon, Raymond, wake up! You're gonna be late for
school!" Raymond Lauriano, eleven, buried his face
deeper into his pillow. But as usual, his brother, Jesse,
didn't stop. He jerked Raymond's bedspread off and
shook his shoulder roughly. "Get *up!*"

Raymond finally rolled over, a sulky look on his
face. "Leave me alone, Jesse. You're not my boss!"

Mornings had never been Raymond's best time. He
stood up and shuffled across the floor, yelping when
he banged his knee against the motorcycle frame on

the floor. He and Jesse found the old Harley David-son frame and dragged it home to decorate their room. They both dreamed of someday owning a *real* Har-ley—one with wheels and a motor. Until then, they would just have to pretend.

Still irritated, Raymond pulled a T-shirt down over his lumpy black hair. Why did his brother have to be so bossy anyway? He was thirteen, not eighteen!

His mother, Guadalupe Cardeñas, was in the kit-chen, humming as she put away the dishes. His little sister and brother were at the table finishing breakfast. They both looked up when Raymond walked in.

"Hi!" Marlene said cheerfully. She was ten, with the same dark hair and eyes as her twin, Charles. They were the youngest of the family's ten children. Only Jesse, Raymond, and the twins were left at home with Mrs. Cardeñas. They lived in a pretty first-floor apart-ment in El Monte, California.

Raymond ignored his sister's greeting. Without a word, he poured himself a bowl of cereal and sat down to eat. Marlene and Charlie looked at each other and shrugged. They were used to Raymond's bad moods in the morning.

Mrs. Cardeñas glanced up at the clock on the wall. "You must hurry, Raymond," she said sternly in Span-ish. "You woke up very late this morning."

Raymond was still grouchy, but he knew better than to talk back to his mother. She was very short, but she was also very strict!

"Orita voy," he said sulkily. "I'm going." Pushing his bowl away, he stomped back down the hall to brush his teeth. He was glaring at his reflection in the bathroom mirror when a trail of toothpaste oozed down his chin and dripped onto his shirt. He angrily threw his toothbrush into the sink. What *was* it about mornings, anyway?

"Raymond!" It was Mrs. Cardeñas again. This time her voice was sharp. "It's time to go!"

On the way out the door, Jesse and the twins stopped to kiss their mother goodbye, but Raymond just brushed past her. He was tired of being treated like a two-year-old. He could take care of himself!

Once he really woke up, though, his mood quickly improved. It happened like that almost every day. Raymond sometimes felt like two different people: the "morning" him and the "regular" him. He wished he could wake up happy in the mornings like everybody else. It made him feel bad when he hurt his mother's feelings. She had always worked very hard to take care of him and all his sisters and brothers.

After school Raymond ran home from Cogswell Elementary. The outside of his apartment building was painted bright pink, so it was easy to see from a long way off. When he got there, he waved to a friend across the courtyard.

"Hey, Eddie!" he yelled. "Want to play later?"

Eddie waved back and then walked over. "Sure. But I have to finish my homework first."

"Well, hurry up. I was thinking about going over to the laundromat to play some video games." The small laundromat was just behind the apartments.

"You got any money?"

"No . . . but maybe we can get lucky and find some. We can check all the washers. Sometimes there are quarters."

Eddie made a face. "I don't think so, but you can come over to my house if you want."

"OK. I'll see you in a few minutes." Trotting up the front steps to his own apartment, Raymond wished for the millionth time that he was rich. He would buy his mother a big, beautiful house with a flower garden and maybe hire a maid. He'd buy Jesse a real motor-cycle. For himself, he just wanted a fancy new guitar. Jesse sometimes let him play on his old guitar, but it sounded pretty bad. It was ugly too. They had tried to make it look better by pasting stickers all over the outside, but it hadn't helped much.

Raymond ran inside and slammed the door. "Mama! I'm home!"

Mrs. Cardeñas hur-ried around the corner from the kitchen and gave him a tired smile.

Raymond plays his brother Jesse's old guitar

"How was school today, Raymond? Did you obey your teachers?"

"*Si*, Mama," Raymond said quickly. "I was fine. But look . . . I'm sorry I was so grouchy this morning."

Mrs. Cardeñas reached over to hug him. "You need to get over your bad temper, *mijo*," she said. *Mijo* means "my son" in Spanish. "Someday it will get you into big trouble."

Raymond nodded. "I know. But I hate mornings. Everybody bothers me." He threw his school bag on the couch. "Can I go over to Eddie's now? He wanted me to play."

"Do you have any homework?"

"No. I finished it all at school."

"Then go. But be sure you are home before dark."

"OK, I will. Bye!" This time, Raymond planted a kiss on her cheek before he left. Maybe it would make up for the way he'd acted that morning.

Raymond watched TV at Eddie's while his friend finished his homework. Then they went outside to sit on the steps. They were talking quietly when Raymond's friend Danny came running up.

"Raymond!" he said breathlessly. "There's some guy over by the car wash with a motorcycle! He said he'd let us ride it! Come on!"

Raymond jumped up. "I'll be back in a few minutes, Eddie. I want to check this out!"

The car wash, the laundromat, and a small food store were all in a shopping center behind the apartments. Raymond followed Danny, excited at the thought of riding a real motorcycle. Jesse would be jealous!

"Who is this guy, Danny?" he asked. "Is he a friend of yours?"

"Yeah, sort of," Danny replied. "I think he lives here in the apartments. His name's Easy."

"Easy? That's a funny name."

"I think it's a nickname. Look, there he is!"

An Exciting New Friend

Raymond saw the motorcycle first. It was a small red Moped. Not exactly a Harley, but at least it had a motor. He slowed to a walk, suddenly feeling shy. Maybe the man had just been teasing about letting them ride it.

But Danny pulled him along. "Come on! Easy's really nice."

A man in his mid-twenties was leaning against the side of the car wash, his arms crossed. He had thick black hair and was wearing jeans and a slightly greasy T-shirt. He smiled when the boys ran up.

"Hey, Easy! This is my friend, Raymond," Danny said. "I told him about your motorcycle."

Easy gave Raymond a friendly nod. "Hi there," he said. "You like motorcycles too?"

"Yeah. Me and my brother have a Harley frame in our room."

"A Harley! That's great." Easy turned to Danny. "I guess you'll be first. You want to take a little ride around the parking lot?"

Danny's eyes lit up. "Sure!"

"Then climb on. I'll show you how to start it."

Raymond sat down on the curb to watch. He laughed as his friend climbed onto the motorcycle seat, trying not to look excited. Easy showed him how to kick the starter pedal down. After several tries, Danny got it started.

Then Easy climbed on behind him. "OK, just watch what I do this time. Then I'll let you try it alone." Reaching around Danny, he twisted the hand-control on the handlebars. The motorcycle jerked and then rolled forward. Danny held on tight as they made several slow loops around the car wash.

Finally, they stopped and Easy got off. "Now let's see if you can do it by yourself. Just take it very slow. Go ahead!"

Danny looked a little scared. "What if I start going too fast?"

"Just put on the brakes. It's not that hard. Trust me."

Danny took a deep breath. "OK. Here goes!" Raymond held his breath, half expecting Danny to fall over or run into something. Instead, he drove around in a big circle, with Easy yelling instructions. After a few more circles, Danny was grinning ear to ear.

"Can I take Raymond for a ride now?" he asked. "I'll be careful."

Easy shrugged. "Why not?"

Raymond looked at his friend doubtfully. "I don't know, Danny. You look like a pretty crazy driver!"

"What are you, chicken? Come on!"

Raymond climbed up behind Danny, holding onto his shirt as Danny drove him in circles around the car wash. Finally, Easy waved for them to stop.

"I think that's probably enough driving for today," he said, smiling. "What else are you guys interested in? You like karate?"

"I do!" Danny said. He made a few chopping motions in the air. "Why?"

"I have this friend who knows karate. He could show you guys some moves. He lives right around the corner."

"That sounds fun! You want to go, Raymond?"

Raymond wanted to, but something made him hesitate. He didn't think his mom would like him going off to somebody else's house like that. He was still thinking about it when Marlene ran up.

"Raymond!" she said, slightly out of breath. "Mama's been calling you. It's dinner time!"

Raymond rolled his eyes. "I guess I have to go now, but thanks anyway."

Easy smiled down at Marlene. "Is this your little sister?"

"Yeah." For some reason, Raymond suddenly felt uncomfortable. "Well, come on Marlene. I'll see you guys later."

On the way back to their apartment, Marlene asked, "Who was that man you were talking to, Raymond? He looked kind of creepy."

"He's a friend of Danny's. He's OK." He gave Marlene a scornful look. "And he doesn't look creepy; he looks cool. Don't you know the difference?"

"He was dirty."

"He'd probably been working on his motorcycle. Forget it, Marlene. You're such a baby."

Raymond hoped his mom wouldn't find out that he'd ridden Easy's motorcycle. She would probably get mad. She didn't like him talking to strangers.

But Easy *wasn't* a stranger, Raymond assured himself. He was a neighbor in the apartments. Besides, he was Danny's friend, and it was really nice of him to let them ride his motorcycle.

Lessons from a Dog's Ear

After dinner, Mrs. Cardeñas called Raymond. Each night she picked a different child to read with her from the family Bible. Afterward they would spend a few minutes talking or playing a game. It was one of the few times the kids got to have her all to themselves.

This time, Mrs. Cardeñas decided to read out of the Book of Proverbs. Raymond didn't listen closely to the words, but he liked the way her voice sounded as she read softly in Spanish. Several of the proverbs made him laugh, like the one that said getting mixed up in someone else's fight was like pulling a dog's ears, or that making the same mistake over and over was like a dog returning to its own vomit. Most of the time they read about Moses and stuff, not about dogs. He decided he liked Proverbs.

Finally, Mrs. Cardeñas closed the big Bible with a thump. "So, *mijo*," she said. "Are things going well with you?"

Raymond shrugged. "Pretty well, Mama. I just wish we had more money. I can't wait until I'm old enough to get a job."

"You will be a man soon enough. We have food to eat and a nice home to live in. We have everything we need. We must be content with that."

Raymond gave a sigh and then said, "But it's boring always being broke! I wanted to go play video games with Eddie today, but I couldn't. I never get to do anything fun."

Mrs. Cardeñas looked troubled. "I worry about you when you talk like that, Raymond. Jesse tells me you get into fights at school, and that some of your friends take part in gangs. You don't always know the difference between fun and danger."

Raymond rolled his eyes. So *that* was why she was reading about staying out of fights! Jesse was such a bigmouth.

"Jesse's just trying to get me in trouble, Mama," he said. "My friends are OK."

"I hope so. You're a smart boy with a bright future. It would be foolish to throw it away. Do you understand?"

"*Si*, Mama. But you worry too much. I can take care of myself." Raymond grinned. "Now why don't we quit talking about this boring stuff? I was hoping you might make some cookies tonight. I'll help if you do. I'll even wash the dishes!"

Mrs. Cardeñas laughed. "OK. But just remember what I told you, Raymond. There are more important things than money and excitement."

"I know, Mama." Shaking his head, Raymond followed her back out to the kitchen. It was always the same thing: "Don't do this. Don't do that. Be careful." His mother worried too much.

If he listened to everything she said, he would probably still be in diapers. Baby Raymond, the only eleven-year-old in the world who wasn't allowed to have fun!

The next afternoon, Raymond was busy playing with other friends while Danny went down the street to the school to practice driving Easy's motorcycle. But when it got dark and Danny still wasn't back, his mom got worried. Danny hadn't told her where he was going. Raymond offered to go find him.

It wasn't hard to spot him. Danny was buzzing noisily around the school parking lot while Easy watched from one side. When Raymond waved, Danny stopped.

"Did you see me?" Danny asked excitedly. "I'm getting really good at this. You want a ride?"

Raymond shook his head. "Your mom sent me to find you. She's been calling you. She didn't know where you were."

"Oh, great," Danny said gloomily. "I'm probably in trouble."

Easy laughed. "My mom's like that too. You'd better head home fast. You don't want to make her worry."

"Do you live with your mom, Easy?" Raymond asked curiously. "Which apartment are you in, anyway?"

"I've been renting a room in a friend's apartment, but they just kicked me out. Now I'm staying with some other friends around the corner." He smiled. "My mom doesn't live around here. I wish she did. She cooks a lot better than me."

Raymond poked Danny in the back to hurry him along. "Well, we have to go. See you later, Easy."

"*Adios!* Be careful going home!"

Running back toward their pink apartments, the two boys talked about their new friend. "He doesn't treat me like a stupid little kid," Danny said. "And he likes to do cool stuff. You know his friend who teaches karate? Easy said he has another friend in Chicago who makes karate movies! He said he might take us there someday to be in a movie."

"That'd be fun. We could be movie stars!" They both giggled.

But for some reason, Raymond still didn't mention Easy at home. The way his mom acted, anybody she didn't know might as well be an axe murderer. She would probably yell at him for even talking to Easy.

He didn't see Easy again until three days later. He was with Danny, looking at baseball cards at the corner store, when he heard a motorcycle pull up outside. It was Easy. A boy about Raymond's age was on the motorcycle seat behind him.

Easy looked happy to see them. "Hi, guys! This is my nephew, Juan. He's from TJ." TJ was short for Tijiuana, Mexico. "He doesn't speak much English. He's staying with me."

Raymond said hello to Juan in Spanish, but the boy didn't say much. Easy finally suggested they all go next door to play video games.

"We don't have any money," Raymond said. "But we'll go watch you guys play."

Easy waved that idea away. "That's no fun! Here. I'll give you each a couple of dollars." He dug in his pocket and came up with a handful of quarters. "Here you go. Take as much as you need."

Danny and Juan quickly scooped up four quarters and ran over to the video games, but Raymond hesitated. He wasn't supposed to take money from people. But they were only quarters. What could it hurt?

"Thanks," he said. As he took four quarters, he noticed Easy's hands for the first time. His fingertips all looked scarred and blistery, like they'd been burned. He thought maybe he'd burned them working on his motorcycle.

Easy gave him a friendly punch on the arm. "You want some candy too? Go ahead and take enough to buy everybody some snacks."

Since Raymond had already taken money for a video game, he didn't see that it made any difference. "OK. I'll get some Red Vines. But I'll pay you back when I get some money."

"Forget it. I have plenty of money."

Raymond bought the candy and then played a few games with Danny and Juan. Easy watched, cheering them on and making jokes whenever they messed up. Finally, he motioned to his nephew that it was time to leave.

"I've got stuff to do," he explained. "I guess I'll see you guys later."

"Thanks for the Red Vines," Raymond said politely.

"No problem. You guys are my friends now, right?"

Raymond nodded, flattered. It made him feel important to have a friend who was older. Even Jesse didn't have a friend with a real motorcycle!

Hanging Out with a New Friend?

At home that evening, it was Marlene's turn for Bible reading. While she and Mrs. Cardeñas were busy with that, Raymond, Jesse, and Charlie watched TV. They were sprawled out on the living room floor when Danny rang the doorbell. Raymond let him in.

"My mom wants to know if your mom can come over for a minute," Danny said. "Is she around?"

"She's doing her Bible reading with Marlene. I'll go get her."

Mrs. Cardeñas went to the neighbor's, saying she'd be back in a few minutes. Danny decided to stay and watch TV with Raymond until she got back.

Almost immediately, the doorbell rang again. This time Marlene jumped up to answer it. A boy stood nervously on the step.

"Is Raymond here?" he asked in Spanish.

"Si," Marlene replied. She turned and shouted over her shoulder, "Raymond? It's somebody for you."

Danny followed Raymond to the door. They were both surprised to see Easy's nephew standing there.

"Easy wants to see you," the boy said quickly. "He said for you to hurry."

"Where is he?"

"In the garage behind the apartments. He just bought another motorcycle. He wants to show it to you."

Raymond hesitated and then said, "OK. But I can't be gone long. I have to be back home by dark."

They found Easy at the garage, but he had the same old motorcycle as before. "The new one's at my friend's house down the street," he explained. "It's only a couple of blocks away. Hop on and I'll take you there.

Raymond, you can sit here in front of me. Juan can ride on back."

Danny looked confused. "Where will I sit?"

"Oh, I'm sorry, Danny. I don't think we can all fit. How about if I bring it over tomorrow and show you?"

Danny turned away, disappointed. "OK. See you tomorrow. Bye, Raymond."

But as soon as Danny was out of sight, Easy changed his mind. "This is too crowded. Why don't you two just follow me on foot? I'll go slow."

Raymond and Juan climbed down again. "How far is it?" Raymond asked. "I have to be back home by dark."

"Not far. Just around the corner."

Easy drove off slowly, leaving Raymond and Juan to trot along behind him. After several blocks, they stopped in front of a house with a motorcycle out front. Raymond started walking over to look at it when Easy grabbed his arm.

"The police!" he gasped, looking back over his shoulder. "Hurry, get on my bike! We've got to get out of here!"

Raymond froze. What was he talking about? There weren't any police around. And even if there were, they weren't doing anything wrong!

But Easy didn't wait for him to obey. With one swift movement, he jerked Raymond up onto the motor-cycle seat in front of him and took off. Juan had already leaped onto the seat behind him.

Raymond was too scared to move as Easy roared down the narrow street and screeched around a corner. What was happening? Without slowing down, they raced down one street after another. Finally, they stopped in front of another house.

"My friend lives here," Easy said. "You guys come inside. I have some business to take care of."

Raymond looked around, wondering where they were. It didn't look familiar, but they couldn't be *too* far from home. They'd only been driving about ten minutes.

"Easy?" he said nervously. "I really need to go home. It's almost night. I'm going to get in trouble."

"This will only take a few minutes. I'll take you home right after that."

Raymond wasn't happy as he followed Easy and his nephew inside the house. His mom was going to be mad if she ever found out about this!

Easy went off to talk to his friend, leaving Raymond and Juan in the living room. But Raymond could hear their voices clearly in the next room.

"Are you going to let me borrow the $200?" Easy asked. "I'll need it to get to Chicago."

"I don't know, man. That's a lot of money."

Raymond looked over at Juan. "Are you guys going to Chicago?" he whispered. The other boy just shrugged. Why didn't he ever talk?

Finally, Raymond couldn't wait any longer. It was completely dark outside. He had to get home! He walked into the next room to talk to Easy.

"I'm sorry to bother you," he said, "but I need to go home. If you're not ready to go, I'll just walk. OK?"

Easy stood up. "You're not going anywhere, Raymond. If the police see you, they'll throw you in jail. They've been looking for me, and now they're looking for you." His friendly smile was gone. Now he just looked mad.

"But I haven't done anything!" Raymond protested. "Why would they put me in jail?"

Easy held out his hands. "See this? The last time the police were after me, I burned off all my fingerprints with acid. You've been with me and that's all that matters. If they find you out by yourself, you'll go straight to jail."

Raymond opened his mouth and then closed it again. Did the police really put kids in jail? He was still wondering about that when Easy spoke again in a softer voice.

"Look, just relax, OK? I won't let anything bad happen to you. You're my friend. I'll take you home in a few minutes. Maybe the police won't find out about you being with me."

Raymond nodded slowly, feeling confused. He wanted to believe Easy, but he wasn't so sure anymore that he was telling the truth. This was all like a bad dream. He went back to the living room to wait.

A few minutes later, Easy appeared. "OK, time to go!" he said cheerfully. Relieved, Raymond followed Easy and his nephew back to the motorcycle. *At last!*

Ten minutes later they were back in Raymond's neighborhood. Raymond felt better when he saw his pink apartments just ahead. He'd been a little afraid that Easy might not take him home after all. He was acting so strange!

But instead of stopping at the apartments, Easy roared on past. Raymond was startled. "Hey!" he shouted. "You passed my house! Go back!"

Easy shook his head. "We're going to my apartment first to pick up some things. Then I'll drop you off."

Raymond's heart sank. He'd been so close! He bit his lip, trying to keep from crying. He should have jumped off and run away when he had the chance. His mom was going to be *mad!*

Easy's apartment was on the bottom floor of a dingy building. Raymond slowly followed him up the walk, wishing he were a million miles away. Why was Easy doing this to him? He looked over at Juan, suddenly wondering about him. Was he really Easy's nephew, or had Easy just said that? There was something funny going on.

To his surprise, two other boys were waiting inside the apartment. Neither of them spoke English. They nodded to Raymond but didn't smile.

Raymond pulled Juan aside. "Who are they?" he asked in a low voice. "What are they doing here?"

For once, the other boy answered. "They ran away from home in TJ. Easy brought them with us."

"Why?"

Juan shrugged. "Easy said he'd buy them motor-cycles and take them on a trip."

Raymond stared at him and then back at the other two boys. How could they have believed a big lie like that? Then he realized he had believed a bunch of lies too. His throat suddenly grew tight.

"I want to go home," he said, his voice shaking. "I don't want to be here. I want to go home!"

Just then, another man arrived with a car. Easy told Raymond and Juan to get in the car. When Raymond balked, Easy said, "You want to go home, don't you?"

"Yes," Raymond said tearfully. "Is that where we're going this time?"

"Sure. We're going to drop you off."

"You promise?"

"I promise. Just get in the car."

But it was soon clear that Easy had tricked him again. They drove all around but never to Raymond's apartments. Finally, when he realized they weren't going to take him home, Raymond started to cry.

Kidnapping Made "Easy"

Raymond didn't know how long they drove before they stopped at a gas station. He cried the whole way. Easy and his friend got out of the car and then Easy stuck his head back inside. "Hey, you guys want some ice cream?"

Juan said yes, but Raymond shook his head. "I j-just want to go h-home," he said between sobs. He had cried so hard that his shirt and jeans were both soaked.

"Sorry. You'd better shut up, Raymond, or you'll end up in jail. You'll make people suspicious, crying like that."

"I c-can't help it!" Raymond said rebelliously. "Take me home!"

Easy ignored him. After buying ice cream and pumping some gas, they took off again. Raymond was crying too hard to notice which direction they were going. But when the car suddenly slowed down again, he sat up and looked around. They were pulling up next to a small red sports car.

In the front seat, Easy said to his friend, "That's the one we want. Stop right here."

Raymond watched in disbelief as Easy jumped out and ran over to the sports car. Within seconds he had the door open and the engine started. *He was stealing it!*

Then Easy dashed back over to his friend's car. He opened the back door and grabbed Raymond by the arm. "You guys are coming with me now. Hurry up!"

Before he could react, Easy had shoved him into the other car. Raymond slumped down in the seat, terrified. If the police caught them now, he'd be in trouble for sure. *A stolen car!* He pressed both hands over his mouth, trying to stop himself from crying. How had he gotten himself into this? When he got home, he was going to tell his mother everything. If he had to go to jail, he would go, but he couldn't let Easy get away with stealing a car!

Easy drove back to his apartment to pick up the other two boys. He made Raymond move up to the front seat to give them more room in the back seat. Raymond started crying so hard that he almost threw up. He finally fell asleep leaning against the car door.

When he woke up hours later it was morning. Outside, he saw mountains.

/ / /

Raymond sat up slowly, rubbing his eyes. They were sore and puffy from crying, and his stomach hurt. "Where are we?" he asked. "Are we still in El Monte?"

"Sure," Easy said. "Are you feeling better now?"

"No." Raymond glanced over at Easy, confused at his sudden friendliness. How could he be so mean one minute and so nice the next? He was like an actor!

He soon got to see what a good actor he really was. When a police car appeared on the highway behind them with its lights flashing, Easy had to pull over. Raymond felt a leap of hope. Maybe he could get away now. What could Easy do with a policeman standing right there?

But Easy must have guessed what he was thinking. "You say one word, Raymond, and you'll go to jail," he hissed. "I'll tell them you helped steal the car. If they ask, you say you're my cousin. Got it?"

Raymond swallowed. "Got it." Suddenly, it didn't seem like such a good idea to tell on Easy. He was half crazy. What if he had a gun?

The policeman walked up to the car and looked inside. "What's the hurry, mister? You trying to kill these kids?"

"No, sir," Easy said. "I just got word that my mom's in the hospital, and we're on our way to Nevada to see her. I guess I wasn't watching my speed."

"Well, you'd better watch it from now on." The policeman wrote out a speeding ticket and tore it off his pad. "We don't want you to wind up in the hospital with your mom."

"No, sir. Thanks."

As the policeman walked back to his car, Easy took a deep breath. "That was close," he said.

Raymond was confused. "Why were you talking about Nevada? I thought you said we were still in El Monte."

"Don't worry about it."

They drove all day, only stopping to buy gas or food. Raymond ignored the three boys in the back seat. They had all come along because they wanted to, not because they had to. He thought they were crazy.

He ignored Easy too, even though he kept trying to cheer him up. But when Easy was being so nice, it was hard to remember that he was a kidnapper. It made Raymond feel confused. After a while he started talking to Easy again. Maybe he wasn't really such a bad guy. He hadn't done anything to hurt him, had he? And he had tried to buy ice cream to make him feel better. Maybe it was just some misunderstanding.

But every time Raymond thought about home, he got upset all over again. His mother would be so worried. She was probably crying and crying, wondering what had happened to him. Jesse and the twins were probably crying too. And what about school? It was Thursday and he was supposed to take a test. Everything was such a mess.

Putting his head down on his knees, the eleven-year-old once again burst into tears.

The Home Search Begins

Back in El Monte, Jesse was sitting in his seventh-grade English class, staring down at his pencil. The night before, when his brother hadn't come home, he had gone everywhere looking for him. By midnight, they all knew something was wrong. Mrs. Cardeñas had called the police.

"Jesse? Would you like to go lie down for a few minutes?" Jesse jumped; his teacher had walked right up beside him without him noticing. She looked sad. She knew all about Raymond. It had been on the news that morning.

"No, thanks. I'm OK." Jesse reached for his pencil, but his hand was shaking too hard for him to pick it up. He pushed it around instead. Where was Raymond? It was hard to think about anything else. Jesse blinked back tears. If anybody had done anything to hurt his brother, he would never rest until they paid for it.

/ / /

For dinner that evening, Easy stopped at a McDonald's and bought burgers and fries for everybody. Raymond sipped a Coke, but he was too upset to eat. All he could think about was how dumb he had been to get into this. By now, his mom probably thought he was dead. He wished he could let her know he was OK, but Easy never let him out of his sight.

They finally stopped in Las Vegas, Nevada, for the night. Easy parked outside a casino, and they all slept in the car. Early the next morning they started off again. Easy planned to cross Utah and reach Colorado by that night.

With each passing mile, Raymond grew sadder and more desperate. He had given up on begging Easy to take him back home. Easy wouldn't tell him why he wanted him, but Raymond was afraid it was for something bad. Otherwise, why would he kidnap him? It didn't make any sense.

That afternoon, when they pulled into a rest stop, Raymond finally saw a chance to get away. Easy went off to use the bathroom, leaving him in the car. The moment Easy was out of sight, Raymond jumped out and looked around. He needed to find help, fast!

There were only a few other cars in the parking lot. One was a van with California license plates. Raymond started toward it.

But he had only taken two steps when someone roughly grabbed his arm. "Where do you think you're going?" Easy demanded furiously. "Get back in the car."

"I was just . . . I just wanted to take a walk," Raymond stammered. "My legs are stiff."

"Too bad." Easy shoved him back into the front seat and slammed the door. A moment later they were roaring back down the highway.

/ / /

Jesse walked slowly along the riverbank, staring down into the weeds. Over the last two days he and his friends had searched everywhere for Raymond: between houses, in alleys, at other apartment buildings. They had found no trace of him. Now, as they searched the river, Jesse prayed his brother wouldn't be there.

The day before, Danny had finally told the police about Easy. From his description, they had drawn a picture to pass out. Since then, many others had joined the search. Kids and old people from the apartments worked side by side. Teenage gang members in the neighborhood volunteered to help the police in their search. Strangers brought food or called to say that they were praying for Raymond. Everybody wanted to help.

Raymond's teacher made "Missing" fliers with Raymond's photograph and passed them out. Jesse rode his bike all over town, putting the posters up in store windows.

But nothing seemed to work. After two days, it was as if Raymond Lauriano had disappeared from the face of the earth.

Cross-Country Flight

It was late that night when they reached Colorado. Easy bought tuna sandwiches at a small market, but Raymond still couldn't eat. He had cried so much that it felt like his throat was glued shut. He was weak and dizzy from not eating, but he couldn't help it. He didn't think he could ever eat again.

They all slept in the car again. The next morning, on Saturday, Raymond listened numbly as Easy explained to the other boys that he was going to sell the car and buy each of them a motorcycle. He was such a liar. How could they believe him?

"I want to go home," Raymond said aloud. He hadn't meant to say it; it just popped out. He knew it wouldn't do any good.

Easy pretended not to understand. "Don't you want a motorcycle of your own, Raymond? I thought you'd like that."

Raymond didn't bother to answer. When they started out again, he looked out the window, reading the license plates on other cars. Most were from Colorado, but some were from Kansas or Nebraska. He wondered if they were going to Kansas next.

They drove all morning and into the afternoon. Raymond had just started noticing Iowa license plates when Easy pulled into another rest stop. He walked over to a pay phone, keeping an eye on Raymond the whole time. When he came back, he looked mad.

"My friend says the police in El Monte are looking for you," he told Raymond. "They even have a $2,000 reward out for you. I need you to write to your mother. Tell her you're OK, and that you'll be back in a month."

"A month?" Raymond cried. "I can't wait that long! I want to go home *now!*"

"Do what I say, or you'll be sorry," Easy snarled. Scared, Raymond agreed to write the letter.

But they had just gotten back on the highway when they heard police sirens. Raymond twisted around in his seat. Two police cars were racing up behind them!

"Quit looking back," Easy snapped. "Maybe they'll go around us." But the police didn't pass them. One stayed right behind them while the other pulled up beside them. The officer motioned for Easy to pull the car over to the side of the road.

Raymond's heart was pounding as Easy stopped the car. One thing he knew for sure; this time, even if Easy shot him, he was going to tell the police the truth. Anything would be better than this!

The minute the car stopped, Raymond jumped out and ran over to the police car. The police officer was startled when Raymond burst into tears.

"Help me!" he cried. "He's lying! I'm not his cousin!"

"Hey, calm down," the officer said. "Everything's OK. What's your name?"

Raymond took a deep breath. "I'm Raymond Lauriano," he said clearly. "I want to go home!"

The officer nodded. Raymond glanced back over his shoulder, half-expecting Easy to be pointing a gun at him. But the other policeman already had Easy up against the side of the car, his hands handcuffed behind his back. Raymond sighed with relief.

"He stole that car," he said shakily. "I saw him, but I didn't help. Do I still have to go to jail?"

The police officer raised an eyebrow. "Of course not! We're here to take you home. You've had lots of people back in El Monte worried." He nodded over toward Easy. "*He's* the one who's going to jail."

"Good!" For the first time in three days, Raymond felt like smiling. It was all over. He was going home.

Three Months Later

"Get out of bed, Raymond! You're going to be late for school!"

Raymond groaned. "OK, Jesse. I'm coming." He rolled over and then yelped as he fell down onto the floor in a tangle of sheets. Jesse burst out laughing, but Raymond just shook his head. Brothers!

He stumbled sleepily out to the kitchen and gave his mom a hug. "Good morning, Mama."

"*Gracias a Dios que amanasieron,*" she said, smiling. That meant, "Thank God, you woke up." It was how she greeted him now every morning. "Did you rest with the angels?"

"*Si.* No bad dreams last night."

Right after the kidnapping, he'd had nightmares almost every night. He'd wake up crying, thinking Easy had come back for him. Jesse always sat and talked with him until he fell back asleep. Now, slowly, the bad dreams were fading.

Easy was safely locked away in jail. He would soon be tried for kidnapping, car theft, and for a lot of other crimes. Raymond never wanted to see him again, but the El Monte police said they needed him to testify at the trial. Raymond agreed to do it; after all, he was part of El Monte's new Junior Police Explorers.

The Junior Police Explorers was one of the many changes that had happened in El Monte since Raymond's kidnapping. After seeing how well everybody had worked together, the police department had formed a citywide youth patrol. Many teens who'd been in gangs had discovered they liked working *with* the police more than against them. They were trained and then given police department T-shirts and caps. Many of the crime problems around El Monte were dropping.

But the biggest change was in Raymond himself.

"The whole time I was gone, I kept remembering all the mean things I'd done, or mean things I'd said to people," he told Jesse later. "I decided if I ever got back home again, I'd never hold another grudge. And I'd start treating everybody a lot nicer.

"I learned," he added, "that you never can tell when it might be your last time to talk to someone you love."

After his conviction, Easy was sentenced to twelve years in prison.

/ / /

(From top: Jesse, Raymond. Bottom: Charlie, Marlene)

John Collmer with his golden retriever Cinnamon

Swept Underground

The John Collmer Story

The eighth-grade English class at Austin Academy had just started when a masked man kicked in the door.

"Shut up, or I'll pull the trigger!" the man snarled. The teacher screamed, and the man waved a sawed-off shotgun at her.

John Collmer, thirteen, was sitting at the front of the class, closest to the door. Without turning his head, he slid his eyes back and forth to see what his classmates were doing. Several were crying; others were ducking down to hide. The teacher, Mrs. Bodine, looked like she was about to faint.

The gunman stepped sideways, closer to John's desk. John could see the sweat on the back of his neck and a small rip in his sleeve. It gave him an idea. If the man moved just a little closer, he could trip him and grab the shotgun!

Holding his breath, John waited. The gunman edged closer.

Finally, John saw his chance. Quick as lightning, he lifted both his feet and—

"John Collmer!" It was Mrs. Bodine. "Are you paying any attention at all to what I'm saying? Or are you daydreaming again?"

John blinked. "Um, yes, ma'am," he said. "I mean, no, ma'am. I mean, I was listening."

"Oh, you were? Then can you tell me what I was just talking about?"

John frowned, trying desperately to think. He hated English. Half the time, even when he was listening, he didn't understand what she was talking about. Math was the only subject he was any good at.

"I forget," he said lamely. His classmates giggled as Mrs. Bodine shook her head. John sank lower in his seat, wishing a real gunman would show up to distract them. He could be a hero instead of a joke!

That's the trouble with school, he thought. Nothing exciting ever happens. In fact, it was the same thing at home. Day after day, week after week, it was all just the same. He wished once—just once!—that he could have some kind of adventure.

/ / /

The next morning, thunder was rumbling when John's alarm went off. He sat up, yawning. Why did it have to go and rain again on Friday? It had been stormy all week. He had hoped the weekend would be nicer. It wasn't usually this rainy in October.

Stumbling downstairs, John shook some pancake mix into a bowl, tossed in an egg and some milk and stirred it until it looked like goo. He then poured two lumpy blobs onto the hot griddle. They sizzled and slowly spread into pancake-ish shapes.

John had been cooking pancakes for his breakfast ever since he was nine. Now, after three years of practice, he was kind of a pancake expert. To be different, he liked to spread them with peanut butter instead of plain butter. It made them taste more interesting.

He was just sliding them onto his plate when his mother rushed in. Mrs. Collmer was a Reading Recovery teacher at Stephens Elementary in Rowlett, Texas, so she always had to leave early. She grabbed her tote bag off the table and then looked around quickly to make sure she wasn't forgetting anything.

Finally she turned to John. "Did you do all your homework?" she asked, as always.

"Yes," John replied. Having a teacher for a mom had some real disadvantages. Homework was very important to her. She *lived* for homework! He felt sorry for the poor little kids in her class.

"Good," Mrs. Collmer said. "Show it to me."

John rolled his eyes. Just because he hadn't finished his homework a few times—well, maybe more than a few times—she always checked on him now. But it didn't do any good to argue with her. She always won.

"It's just one page of algebra," he grumbled. "If you want to see it, it's in my backpack."

After checking to make sure it was really there, Mrs. Collmer tucked the paper back into his math folder. "OK, thanks. I've got to go now. You work hard in school today, OK?"

"Uh-huh. Bye, Mom."

John always enjoyed having the house to himself after his parents left for work. Julie, his eighteen-year-old sister, was still at home, but he never saw her in the morning. She didn't get up until after he went to school.

John was just finishing his peanut butter pancakes when a large, wet nose nudged his elbow. He looked down to see Cinnamon, his sister's fat golden retriever, staring up at him. He grinned and patted her head.

"Here you go, girl," he said, putting the sticky peanut-butter-and-syrup plate down on the floor. The dog gobbled up the last bite of pancake and then slurped up all the syrup. When the plate was clean, she looked up at John and wagged her tail hopefully.

"Sorry, that's it," he said. "Besides, you're already too fat. You're going to have to go to Doggy Weight Watchers if you don't watch out."

Cinnamon was supposed to be a family dog, but she had always liked Julie best. Julie talked to her a lot, telling her all about her day or sharing secrets about her current boyfriend. John thought it was pretty strange, her talking to a dog like that. But then again, *Julie* was pretty strange! Why else would she have dumped Corey, her only boyfriend John had actually *liked?*

By the time John went out to wait for the bus, it was starting to rain. He shouldered his backpack with a sigh. He hated being stuck indoors over the weekend when he could be doing things like playing basketball or going fossil hunting. He especially liked fossil hunting. He and his dad had filled the big glass case in their living room with shark's teeth, stone arrowheads, and mosasaur bones they'd found. He had been hoping they could go fossil hunting again this weekend.

Then he remembered—tonight was the Dallas Mavericks practice! The day before, his dad had come home with a big surprise: a Mavericks twelve-game ticket package. Tonight was the last open practice of the season. John's three favorite players, Jim Jackson, Jason Kidd, and Jamal Mashburn, would all be there. He couldn't wait.

Bus #523 pulled up with a screech of brakes. The driver, Ms. Luther, was a skinny redhead. She gave

John a sharp look as he climbed on. A few days earlier, she had given him an Office Referral when she caught him eating a candy bar on the bus. John had learned his lesson. Now he only ate candy bars when she wasn't looking.

As the bus rumbled off again, John lurched down the aisle to slide into the seat beside Peter, his best friend.

"Hi," he said.

"Hi," Peter replied. He was skinny with dark hair and also thirteen years old.

John stretched. "How's it going?"

"OK, I guess."

John and Peter always had these exciting conversations in the morning. Later, after they woke up a little, they sometimes thought of better things to talk about.

Playing in the Rain

The day at Austin Academy passed slowly for John, as usual. When the rain became a downpour, John gave up the idea of going fossil hunting that weekend. Heavy rain always turned the creekbeds and fields to thick, slippery mud.

It was still raining when school let out. On the bus home, John and Peter stared glumly out the foggy windows.

"You feel like playing football in the rain?" Peter asked. "We can probably get Chris to play."

John shrugged. "Sure. I'll just go home and get my bike."

His mother and sister were both home. John ran in and slammed the front door to get their attention. "Mom!" he yelled. "I'm going over to Peter's!"

Mrs. Collmer was somewhere downstairs. "OK!" she called. "But remember about the Mavericks practice tonight. You can't be late!"

"I'll remember. Bye!"

John went out through the garage to get his bike. Cinnamon trotted out after him. When he paused to scratch behind her ears, she gave him a big doggy grin, her tongue hanging sideways out of her mouth.

It was still sprinkling outside as John opened the garage. The alley behind his house looked like a small river, with water rushing past. Jumping on his bike, he rode right down the middle of the alley, letting water splash up on both sides. Cinnamon waded along right behind him. Golden retrievers like water.

During the three-block ride to Peter's house, John was surprised at how flooded all the streets were. It must have rained pretty hard the whole time they were in school. He swerved to splash through all the deepest puddles. It was fun riding in the rain!

When he got to Peter's house, his friend came out eating a Twinkie. "Let's go over to Chris's," he said, cheeks bulging. "He's got the football."

"You gonna get your bike?" John asked.

"Nah. I'll just walk."

John rode slowly so Peter and Cinnamon could keep up on foot. They zigzagged through several alleys until they reached the one next to the big, open field where they sometimes played. When they saw the field, they both stared. It looked like a big lake!

"Wow!" Peter said. "Look how much water is out there! Do you think it's deep enough to swim in?"

John shrugged. "Probably."

Peter's eyes got a sudden twinkle. "I'll race you! First one in wins."

John peddled a few more feet, pretending not to be interested. Then, without warning, he dropped his bike and started running. "Gotcha!" he shouted gleefully. Cinnamon raced along behind him, her tongue flapping.

"No fair!" Peter yelled, laughing. He took off after them.

John glanced back over his shoulder. Peter was catching up! There was only one way to beat him.

Reaching the edge of the flooded field, John held his arms out in front of him and dove in headfirst. He didn't hear Peter's sharp warning.

/ / /

Skidding to a halt at the edge of the alley, Peter watched his friend dive into the muddy water. An instant before, a man standing in a driveway nearby had yelled, "Hey, stay out of there! There's a storm drain!"

Peter had shouted for John to stop, but John hadn't heard. Cinnamon had splashed into the water right behind him. Now they were swimming toward the deeper water off to one side. Of course, it wasn't *that* deep; maybe two or three feet at most. If John stood up, it would probably only come to his knees or thighs.

But as Peter watched, it looked like John and Cinnamon were moving sideways in the water. John started splashing harder—like he was trying to fight a current. Cinnamon was also fighting, swimming as hard as she could. What was happening to them?

"Hey!" Peter yelled. "John, come back!"

John turned and lifted one hand over his head. "Help!" he gasped.

The next instant, boy and dog both disappeared beneath the muddy water.

A Watery Nightmare

John had been laughing as he swam, pleased that he had tricked Peter. The water felt good, even though it was muddy. His mom might be mad about him swimming in his clothes and shoes, but it was worth it. It hadn't turned out to be such a boring day after all.

He was splashing along, Cinnamon bobbing at his side, when he felt something gently tugging at his legs. It felt like an underwater current, but that didn't make sense. The water wasn't moving. It was just a big, quiet lake in an empty field. John kicked hard, trying to swim forward. Instead, to his surprise, he was pulled sideways—fast!

Suddenly, the current was much stronger. Instead of sweeping him sideways, it was now sucking him *down!*

Startled, John kicked harder. He still wasn't panicked, though. After all, how bad could the current be in an old flooded field? He was too busy to notice that Cinnamon was also struggling just a few feet away.

But he soon realized he wasn't getting anywhere. Even swimming as hard as he could, he could hardly keep his face above water. Suddenly scared, he twisted around to look for Peter. Peter was standing at the edge of the field, shouting something. John raised his hand.

"Peter!" he tried to shout, but he choked on the water. Swimming frantically, he tilted his head backward to catch a quick breath. He was going under!

"Help!" he sputtered. *"Help!"* He was still yelling when the muddy water closed over his head.

/ / /

The next few seconds were dark confusion. Blinded by the muddy water, John was still thrashing around when something slammed into his head. The blow left him stunned and dizzy. Barely conscious, he let the water sweep him along. He hardly noticed his arms and legs scraping against rough concrete on all sides.

He was lying on his back, shooting feet first down some kind of dark, narrow pipe.

It wasn't until he felt a wet paw frantically clawing the water next to his ear that he snapped out of his daze.

Cinnamon!

He quickly reached back to grab both the dog's paws. He had to get Cinnamon out of here! His sister would be mad if he let her get killed. It didn't occur to John at the time that if Cinnamon died, he probably would too.

Air.

He had always been a strong swimmer. In their backyard pool, John could hold his breath longer than just about anybody. But now his lungs were bursting. He needed to breathe!

Maybe there's an air pocket, he thought. Bracing his basketball shoes against the rough walls on either side, he slowed down long enough to discover that the small pipe—or whatever it was—was completely filled with water. There was no air pocket above him.

That thought was just sinking in when John's right foot caught on something sticking out of the wall. Instantly, his leg bent backwards, toward his head. Pain exploded in his knee as the heel of his basketball shoe touched the right side of his face. It felt like his leg had been twisted off.

In his pain, John lost his grip on Cinnamon's paws. His lungs were now burning. In another few seconds, he would *have* to breathe.

I'm going to die, he thought faintly. Black spots were starting to swirl around in front of his eyes. He wondered what death would be like. He hoped it would be quick and not hurt a lot. Then he thought about his mom. She was going to be so upset when she found out . . .

/ / /

Peter stood in the alley like a statue, his eyes glued to the muddy water. *Come on, John*, he silently cried. *Come back up!*

But when after fifteen long seconds, his friend had still not reappeared, Peter wheeled around in a panic. He had to get help! He ran over and picked up John's bike.

The man who had yelled the warning was already dialing a cellular phone. "I'm calling 911!" he said. Peter nodded and then took off on John's bike. He had to get Mrs. Collmer!

The ride to John's house had never seemed so long. Peter stood on the pedals, pumping as hard as he could. Tears kept mixing with rain, making his eyes blurry. When he finally got to the Collmer's house, he rode right up into the front yard. He jabbed at the doorbell and then banged on the door with both fists.

"Mrs. Collmer!" he called. "Mrs. Collmer, come quick!"

Julie and her mom were in the kitchen cooking dinner when all the banging started. Julie peeked around the corner to see who was at the door. Seeing Peter through the glass, she yelled, "John's not here Peter!"

But he kept banging, and finally Julie and her mom went to the door. As soon as they saw Peter's tear-streaked face, they knew something was wrong.

"It's John," Peter said breathlessly. "He got sucked down a drain or something in that field over by Camelot Street. You've got to come quick!"

Julie's face turned ashen. "I'll drive, Mom. Let's go."

Just in Time

John was just seconds from drowning when the narrow drain pipe suddenly widened. Using the last of his strength, he thrust his face upward, praying he'd find air. His nose and forehead scraped painfully against the rough concrete pipe—but a small pocket of air was trapped there. He gulped it in, almost sobbing with the effort.

Once he had air in his lungs, John's mind grew clearer. He took another deep breath and then leaned his head back in the water. As long as he could find air at the top of the pipe, he could survive. His face might get scraped off, but he'd survive.

Then he remembered Cinnamon. Where was she?

Shooting feet-first down the pipe, his eyes filled with water, John couldn't see anything. He felt above his head, but Cinnamon wasn't there. Had she already drowned? If so, it was all his fault. He had gotten her into this.

Don't think about that, he told himself. He lifted his head to take another breath. The tiny air pocket at the top of the pipe was still there. Maybe I'll make it out OK, at least. . . . If the tiny air pocket stays here. . . .

If the pipe doesn't turn narrow again.

If I don't get knocked out by hitting my head again.

If . . . if . . . if . . . He shoved the gloomy thoughts from his mind. He was going to make it out. He had to. His mom would hyperventilate if he didn't. Somehow, he would get out of this.

But how?

John tried to picture where he was. He knew now that he must be down inside some sort of drainage pipe. He didn't remember ever seeing a pipe in the field, but it must be there. He tried to think about where it was taking him. Was this the pipe that dumped out into Lake Ray Hubbard?

Just then, a blurry slit of light flashed by up to his left. At the same moment a torrent of water poured down like a waterfall, slamming John's sore right leg into the rough concrete. What was going on?

Then he recognized the odd slit shape. It was a street drain, dumping flood water down into the storm sewer!

The light must be daylight, he thought. Somewhere above him was the outside world. Knowing that made him feel better.

But only for a moment. His arms, legs, and face were cut and scraped, and his shirt and shorts shredded. His right leg and knee throbbed. His head ached where he had banged it. He had no way of telling how long it had been since he got sucked down the drain or how far he had gone. After he passed another street drain he tried counting them, but that didn't help. He couldn't remember if there were one or two drains on each block. Every time he had to take a breath, his face got even more scraped up. He was afraid every time that the air pocket above him would disappear.

He had almost given up when the pipe widened again. John lifted his head carefully and then half sat up in the water. A large, round opening was straight ahead—filled with daylight!

"Hey!" he yelled, excited. The next instant, he shot out over Lake Ray Hubbard on a roaring geyser of muddy water.

To his surprise, he saw Cinnamon flying through the air in front of him. She twisted in mid-air and then hit the water, landing on her side. John tumbled in right behind her. Sputtering, he clawed his way back to the surface.

Cinnamon was alive, already swimming toward shore. John quickly caught up with her. "Good girl, Cinnamon!" he said, swimming beside her. But when they reached the riverbank, Cinnamon couldn't climb it. It was too steep and muddy. John got behind her and pushed until she was able to scramble out onto the grass. He wearily crawled up after her.

Cinnamon was waiting for him. She looked terrible. Her face and ears were raw and bleeding, and whole patches of her long, red-gold fur were missing. When she tried to walk, she whined and limped.

"You're going to be OK," John said, patting her gently. "Come on, let's go home."

It wasn't until he took a step that John found that he was limping too. He looked down at himself. He was solid mud and blood. He glanced back at the lake, seeing that the water from the drainage pipe was still shooting out like a waterfall. He suddenly shivered.

He and Cinnamon had been lucky, he realized with awe—very, very lucky.

/ / /

Julie was standing beside her mom, listening as the police talked back and forth on their radios. They were working their way slowly down the street, checking all the storm drains. Mrs. Collmer was crying.

Suddenly, one of the police officers ran up to them, a radio in his hand. "They found him!" he said. "They just called and said he's down on Camelot Street."

Julie gasped. "Is he alive?" She put her arm tighter around her mother's shoulders. For once, she was the strong one.

"Just get in the car," the officer said. "Let's go!"

When they got back to Camelot Street, Julie jumped out. John was sitting in a car, alive! She ran over to him, crying with relief. But when she saw how bloody he was, she didn't try to hug him. He looked like somebody had beaten him with a baseball bat.

"I went home, but nobody was there," John said tiredly. "Cinnamon's OK."

Mrs. Collmer almost collapsed when she saw him. The ambulance workers who were helping John into the ambulance had to stop and help Mrs. Collmer instead. She was so hysterical that she was having trouble breathing. On the way to the hospital, they had to use the siren—not because of John but because of Mrs. Collmer!

At the hospital, after she finally calmed down, John couldn't resist teasing, "You know, Mom, I kept thinking the whole time that you were going to hyperventilate if anything happened to me. But I'm OK now, and you're *still* hyperventilating!"

Back at home that night, the Collmers saw a news story on TV about another boy in a nearby town who had died that same afternoon. He had been playing with some friends in a flooded street by his house when he was sucked down a storm sewer.

John had been lucky. The other boy hadn't.

Adventure Isn't Everything

It took three or four weeks for all John's cuts and bruises to heal. But it took much longer for him to get over what had almost happened. Although he didn't like talking about it, his close brush with death had left him scared.

The first few nights after the accident, he slept in his parents' room, not wanting to be alone. He often woke up screaming, dreaming he was back in the drain pipe. Thunderstorms made him and Cinnamon both nervous. When it rained, they both avoided puddles.

But even though his terrifying trip over half a mile through the underground pipe left John with some scars and bad memories, it did make at least a *few* good things happen.

Several weeks after the accident, the Collmers got a letter from the Mavericks offering them court side seats at their next game. Later, John was selected as an Honorary Ballboy and had his picture taken with both Jim Jackson and Jason Kidd. John framed the autographed picture and put it on his dresser where he could look at it every day.

After his close call in being swept through a storm drain, John Collmer meets one of his favorite Dallas Mavericks, Jim Jackson, during a practice session. (Photo by Layne Murdoch.)

Still, if he had to get swept down into a storm sewer all over again to get that picture, would he do it?

John has a quick answer for that. "The only water pipes I want to go inside from now on are at Wet 'n Wild," he says. "At least there, you know you'll come out safe at the bottom."

/ / /

Do You Have a Real Kids, Real Adventures *Story?*

We're looking for TRUE stories for future volumes of *Real Kids, Real Adventures*—stories about real kids ages nine to seventeen who have faced danger or crisis with extraordinary courage or sometimes become real life heroes. If you have heard about such a story, we might like to use it. The first person to submit a story that we use will have his or her name mentioned in the book and will receive a free copy of that book when it is published.

Please send your story ideas to: Real Kids, Real Adventures, P.O. Box 461572, Garland, TX 75046-1572. Please include your name, address, phone number with area code, and a newspaper clipping with the name and date of the paper, and/or factual information we can use to research the story.

/ / /